D1476782

FOCUS POCUS

GUIDED REFLECTIONS for INTENTION and MINDFULNESS

KIMOTHY JOY

16-MONTH WEEKLY/MONTHLY PLANNER
SEPTEMBER 2022 – DECEMBER 2023

Andrews McMeel
PUBLISHING®

Focus Pocus: Guided Reflections for Intention and Mindfulness
16-Month Weekly/Monthly Planner © 2022 by Kimothy Joy
Printed in China. No part of this calendar may be used or reproduced
in any manner whatsoever without written permission except in
the case of reprints in the context of reviews. For information write
Andrews McMeel Publishing, a division of Andrews McMeel Universal,
1130 Walnut Street, Kansas City, Missouri 64106.

Phases of the moon and start dates for the seasons of the year
are presented in Universal Time.

Every effort has been made to ensure the accuracy of listed holiday
dates; however, some may have changed after publication for official
or cultural reasons.

www.kimothyjoy.com
www.andrewsmcmeel.com

ISBN: 978-1-5248-7359-2

How To Use This Planner

There's a saying, "Where our attention goes, energy flows." Understanding the magnitude of this statement and applying it to our everyday lives can lead to powerful transformation.

I believe it all begins with focus. Years ago, I heard the phrase "focus pocus" in an Abraham-Hicks lecture, and it quickly became my mantra. As a society, we've become masters at the art of distraction. Without making a conscious effort to be more mindful on a daily basis, our energy is scattered. We move at such a fast pace that there seems to be no time to slow down and reflect. We don't take time to listen to ourselves long enough to even know what we really want. This can cause overwhelm, anxiety, and an overall lack of progress toward our goals. We might even wake up thinking, "Wait . . . how did I get here? How did this become my life?" Believe me, I've been there.

This is a manifestation, years in the making, from me to you. This ritual has anchored me through rough waters and has helped me to direct my attention toward my goals consistently, creating a wave of momentum from week to week.

It's a daily journaling and reflection practice comprised of eight prompts that include enriching mindfulness techniques like gratitude list-making, compassionate self-talk, releasing limiting behaviors and thoughts, intention-setting, visualization, and affirmations. It's an invitation to approach each week listening to your inner guidance system, being in the present moment, and exercising your abilities to create your reality from a place of love and compassion. Use this in the way that works best for you! Spend 10-20 minutes at the beginning of each week reflecting and responding to each prompt or choose a prompt per day over the course of the week. Make it your own! Have fun with it. Express yourself to the fullest on each page. And be sure to celebrate and acknowledge your expansion along the way.

The prompts are potent yet only scratch the surface of these powerful techniques as they each have extensive teachings, wisdom, and histories behind them. I invite you to take a deeper dive into those that resonate with you.

We have so much more power to influence our reality than we think we do. I also believe that there is a universal intelligence—insert whatever you want to call this divine presence—we can tap into at any time for support and unconditional love. That's why I'm so eager to share this with you. I know that you, too, are a powerful creative being with limitless potential, eternally supported by a higher force, and you are here to live a life you love.

Appreciate the Good

"I send the following blessings to others and to the world . . ."

We are all connected at the energetic level. Creating a better world begins with each of us actively using our intention and manifestation abilities to do so. Take time to send out loving-kindness to others.

"I am grateful for . . ."

Gratitude list-making has become a popular mindfulness technique for a reason: it's simple and it works. The psychological benefits are endless. If you're in a state of gratitude, you cannot simultaneously be experiencing fear, worry, and angst. Being in the present moment and in a state of appreciation raises your vibration. In minutes it can shift your mindset from lack, scarcity, and fear into abundance, grace, awe, and possibility. As you appreciate who you are and what you already have, you come to understand what fulfills you. Then you can intentionally seek more of it.

Love Myself Deeply

"I am proud of myself for . . ."

Loving and accepting your whole self, even the parts you hide or are ashamed of is an ongoing process and the foundation of creating a deeply fulfilling life. If you don't like who you are, you'll likely end up looking to others and external sources to make you happy. If you truly believe that you are worthy of what you desire, you can break through self-sabotage, doubt, and limited thinking that can lead to procrastination and inaction. Like a muscle that strengthens over time, practicing kind, compassionate self-talk will feel more natural as you go. Start with listing out reasons you're proud to be YOU.

"I am letting go of . . ."

This is a space to be brave and get curious about aspects of yourself that you are ready to release or heal. Gently exploring both the shadow and light aspects of who you are is important to cultivate authentic self-acceptance. Consider reoccurring thoughts you have that may be causing you shame, suffering, or self-sabotage. Do some mental housecleaning and look at where you may need to release a thought, belief, or habit. This can even mean beginning to let go of a person or situation in your life. Write it out. Do it with love and compassion. Ask for assistance and guidance from the universe to support you in doing so. If needed, commit to taking a necessary action to let go.

Manifest and Attract

"I listen deeply then ask clearly for my heart's desires. I am manifesting . . ."

Get clear and ask for what you truly want. You might start by asking yourself the following questions: *What do I really want? What does my soul need? What do I want to experience? How do I want to feel? What resources, support, or people do I want to attract?*

Am I yearning for this from a place of love or fear? Why do I want this? Consider what might bring you long-term fulfillment and joy versus temporary happiness. After this inquiry, write out what comes to mind. It can be general and global or as specific and practical as you want it to be. Make sure it feels good to you. Lastly, ask that it come to fruition for your highest good and the highest good of others.

Here are some examples:
A calm, loving presence. Protecting my inner peace.
Writing my book by January with joy, fun, and ease.
Accepting and loving my body through more rest and movement.

Visualize it

Now focus on feeling it! This is where the untapped power of the imagination comes into play. Take three deep cleansing breaths. For 3-5 minutes, perhaps with headphones on listening to meditation music, use all of your senses to envision your dreams and desires coming to life, like playing a mental movie where you are the director. This practice should evoke powerful, positive emotions that motivate you to keep moving toward your goals. We're already visualizing throughout the day, but without awareness, we often visualize everything that could go wrong or replay past mistakes! Don't skip this step—and trust that if it doesn't come easy at first, you'll get better at it in time. Athletes, leaders, actors, and many others use visualization techniques consistently because it is a proven way to influence the subconscious into believing the event is actually occurring. By mentally enacting your dreams, you will start to look for everyday opportunities to make them your reality. As Muhammad Ali famously stated, *"If my mind can conceive it and my heart can believe it—then I can achieve it."*

Take Inspired Action

Reinforce your intention by committing to taking a physical, concrete action each week that will help you make progress. It can be broad or detailed. Perhaps you have a long-term goal in mind but choose to take more specific action from week to week. The keyword is "inspired" action, so make sure it feels energizing and achievable.

Word or Affirmation I Will Focus On To Keep My Dream Alive

Finally, galvanize your energy and desires into a powerful word or affirmation you can focus on for the week. Write it down in the circle. Look at it and repeat it often. You can choose to write it at the beginning of the week to set the stage for how you want to feel or how you want things to go or choose to write it down after you've filled in the other prompts to help tie everything together. Select words that comfort and uplift you! Get specific or stay general. Don't use affirmations that create inner tension because they feel so far from reality. Remove any words that feel like they put a distance between you and the manifestation. Use active language like "I am, I can, I feel, and I have" instead of words like, "I want, I will, I'll try, I'm going to." Play around with different expressions until it feels right. As Florence Scovel Shinn said, *"Your word is your wand."* Now, focus pocus!

AFFIRMATIONS

Affirmations are power statements that can help us quiet the relentless inner critic and lower the volume on those challenging or distracting thoughts. This fosters healthier self-talk that, according to neuroscientific research, can not only reduce stress but also shift our entire perception of reality. The trick is to actually practice them regularly to experience the long-term benefits. Reciting them may feel awkward at first, but great transformation can occur when we normalize speaking kindly toward ourselves versus defaulting to being unloving and overly critical.

Here are some examples of powerful affirmations:
I am joy. I am ease.
I am safe and protected.
I move through every situation with strength, grace, and patience.
I give myself space to grieve.
I trust that what is meant for me will come to me.
I say no when I need to.
I give myself permission to go slow and rest.
I trust and follow my inner guidance.
I am divinely guided.
I surrender and go with the flow.
I am enough. I do enough. I have enough.
I love my body and accept it fully.
I have abundant health and energy.
I forgive myself.
I feel my emotions with nonjudgment and nonattachment.
I do wonderful work for wonderful pay.
I speak my truth. My voice matters.
I speak up for myself. I speak up for others.
I trust the process and trust my path.
I am worthy of my dreams.

New Moon Ritual

The new moon is potent for amplifying intentions. It's known to be a time of new beginnings and ripe for planting seeds like starting new projects, relationships, and opening ourselves up to new possibilities.

Make a plan ahead of time, then enact it. Start by creating a calm, sacred space. Next, think about your overarching intention for the month and what you'd like to invite into your life. Focus on how you want to feel. Declare your intention on paper or aloud. Once your intention is declared, take physical action that symbolizes this desire or dream (see a list of suggestions below). Finally, release and surrender your request to the universe. Ask that it be done for your highest good and the good of others.

Your rituals can be as simple or elaborate as you'd like them to be. You can do the same ones each month or create a new one each time.

Here are some ideas:
Meditate or pray;
Journal, draw, or paint;
Dance;
Write a song and sing it or play music;
Sit outside in nature;
Go on a mindful walk or hike;
Swim in natural waters.

New Moon Dates (UTC):

September 25, 2022	May 19, 2023
October 25, 2022	June 18, 2023
November 23, 2022	July 17, 2023
December 23, 2022	August 16, 2023
January 21, 2023	September 15, 2023
February 20, 2023	October 14, 2023
March 21, 2023	November 13, 2023
April 20, 2023	December 12, 2023

FULL MOON RITUAL

As we invite new possibilities into our life, we must also practice letting go. The full moon is a ripe time for releasing and clearing what no longer serves us so that we may make space for what does.

Write out everything you're ready to let go of or heal. In a separate list, write out what you are inviting in to replace the first list. Place the "Letting Go" list into a fire (safely) or a bowl of water and watch it dissolve, just like the old habits, behaviors, and beliefs you are releasing. Once the list is gone, cleanse and renew yourself with a walk in the moonlight, a hot bath in salt water, or a different ritual that rejuvenates you.

Full Moon Dates (UTC):

September 10, 2022

October 9, 2022

November 8, 2022

December 8, 2022

January 6, 2023

February 5, 2023

March 7, 2023

April 6, 2023

May 5, 2023

June 4, 2023

July 3, 2023

August 1, 2023

August 31, 2023

September 29, 2023

October 28, 2023

November 27, 2023

December 27, 2023

2023

JANUARY
S	M	T	W	T	F	S
1	2	3	4	5	6	7
8	9	10	11	12	13	14
15	16	17	18	19	20	21
22	23	24	25	26	27	28
29	30	31				

FEBRUARY
S	M	T	W	T	F	S
			1	2	3	4
5	6	7	8	9	10	11
12	13	14	15	16	17	18
19	20	21	22	23	24	25
26	27	28				

MARCH
S	M	T	W	T	F	S
			1	2	3	4
5	6	7	8	9	10	11
12	13	14	15	16	17	18
19	20	21	22	23	24	25
26	27	28	29	30	31	

APRIL
S	M	T	W	T	F	S
						1
2	3	4	5	6	7	8
9	10	11	12	13	14	15
16	17	18	19	20	21	22
23	24	25	26	27	28	29
30						

MAY
S	M	T	W	T	F	S
	1	2	3	4	5	6
7	8	9	10	11	12	13
14	15	16	17	18	19	20
21	22	23	24	25	26	27
28	29	30	31			

JUNE
S	M	T	W	T	F	S
				1	2	3
4	5	6	7	8	9	10
11	12	13	14	15	16	17
18	19	20	21	22	23	24
25	26	27	28	29	30	

JULY
S	M	T	W	T	F	S
						1
2	3	4	5	6	7	8
9	10	11	12	13	14	15
16	17	18	19	20	21	22
23	24	25	26	27	28	29
30	31					

AUGUST
S	M	T	W	T	F	S
		1	2	3	4	5
6	7	8	9	10	11	12
13	14	15	16	17	18	19
20	21	22	23	24	25	26
27	28	29	30	31		

SEPTEMBER
S	M	T	W	T	F	S
					1	2
3	4	5	6	7	8	9
10	11	12	13	14	15	16
17	18	19	20	21	22	23
24	25	26	27	28	29	30

OCTOBER
S	M	T	W	T	F	S
1	2	3	4	5	6	7
8	9	10	11	12	13	14
15	16	17	18	19	20	21
22	23	24	25	26	27	28
29	30	31				

NOVEMBER
S	M	T	W	T	F	S
			1	2	3	4
5	6	7	8	9	10	11
12	13	14	15	16	17	18
19	20	21	22	23	24	25
26	27	28	29	30		

DECEMBER
S	M	T	W	T	F	S
					1	2
3	4	5	6	7	8	9
10	11	12	13	14	15	16
17	18	19	20	21	22	23
24	25	26	27	28	29	30
31						

SepTeMBeR 2022

SUN	MON	TUE	WED	THU	FRI	SAT
				1	2	3
						◑ First Quarter
4	5	6	7	8	9	10
Father's Day (Australia, NZ)	Labor Day (USA, Canada)					○ Full Moon
11	12	13	14	15	16	17
						◐ Last Quarter
18	19	20	21	22	23	24
			U.N. International Day of Peace		Autumnal Equinox	
25	26	27	28	29	30	
● New Moon Rosh Hashanah (begins at sundown)	Queen's Birthday (Australia—WA)	Rosh Hashanah ends				

OCTOBER 2022

SUN	MON	TUE	WED	THU	FRI	SAT
						1
2	3 ◐ First Quarter Labour Day (Australia—ACT, SA, NSW) Queen's Birthday (Australia—QLD)	4 Yom Kippur (begins at sundown)	5	6	7	8
9 O Full Moon	10 Columbus Day (USA) Indigenous Peoples' Day (USA) Thanksgiving (Canada)	11	12	13	14	15
16	17 ◑ Last Quarter	18	19	20	21	22
23	24 Diwali United Nations Day Labour Day (NZ)	25	26	27	28	29
30	31 Halloween Bank Holiday (Ireland)	● New Moon				

November 2022

SUN	MON	TUE	WED	THU	FRI	SAT
		1	2	3	4	5
		◑ First Quarter				
6	7	8	9	10	11	12
Daylight Saving Time ends (USA, Canada)		○ Full Moon Election Day (USA)			Veterans Day (USA) Remembrance Day (Canada, UK, Ireland, Australia)	
13	14	15	16	17	18	19
Remembrance Sunday (UK, Ireland)			◑ Last Quarter			
20	21	22	23	24	25	26
			● New Moon	Thanksgiving (USA)		
27	28	29	30			
			◑ First Quarter St. Andrew's Day (UK)			

DeCemBeR 2022

SUN	MON	TUE	WED	THU	FRi	SAT
				1	2	3
4	5	6	7	8 ○ Full Moon	9 Human Rights Day	10
11	12	13	14	15	16 ◗ Last Quarter	17
18 Hanukkah (begins at sundown)	19	20	21 Winter Solstice	22	23 ● New Moon	24 Christmas Eve
25 Christmas Day	26 Kwanzaa begins (USA) Hanukkah ends Christmas Day (observed) (Australia—NT, SA, WA) Boxing Day (Canada, NZ, UK, Australia—except NT, SA, WA) St. Stephen's Day (Ireland)	27 Christmas Day (observed) (NZ, UK, Australia—except NT, SA, WA) Boxing Day (observed) (Australia—NT, WA) Proclamation Day (observed) (Australia—SA)	28	29	30 ◑ First Quarter	31

JaNuaRY 2023

SUN	MON	TUE	WED	THU	FRI	SAT
1 New Year's Day Kwanzaa ends (USA)	2 New Year's Day (observed) (NZ, Australia, UK)	3 Bank Holiday (UK—Scotland)	4	5	6 ○ Full Moon	7
8	9	10	11	12	13	14
15 ◑ Last Quarter	16 Martin Luther King Jr. Day (USA)	17	18	19	20	21 ● New Moon
22 Lunar New Year (Year of the Rabbit)	23	24	25	26 Australia Day	27	28 ◐ First Quarter
29	30	31				

FeBRuaRY 2023

SUN	MON	TUE	WED	THU	FRI	SAT
			1	2	3	4
5	6	7	8	9	10	11
○ Full Moon	Waitangi Day (NZ)					
12	13	14	15	16	17	18
	◑ Last Quarter	St. Valentine's Day				
19	20	21	22	23	24	25
	● New Moon Presidents' Day (USA)		Ash Wednesday			
26	27	28				
	◐ First Quarter					

MaRCH 2023

SUN	MON	TUE	WED	THU	FRI	SAT
			1 St. David's Day (UK)	2	3	4
5	6 Purim (begins at sundown) Labour Day (Australia—WA)	7 ○ Full Moon	8 International Women's Day	9	10	11
12 Daylight Saving Time begins (USA, Canada)	13 Eight Hours Day (Australia—TAS) Labour Day (Australia—VIC) Commonwealth Day (Australia, Canada, NZ, UK)	14	15 ◑ Last Quarter	16	17 St. Patrick's Day	18
19 Mothering Sunday (Ireland, UK)	20 Vernal Equinox	21 ● New Moon	22 Ramadan	23	24	25
26	27	28	29 ◐ First Quarter	30	31	

APRIL 2023

SUN	MON	TUE	WED	THU	FRi	SAT
						1
2 Palm Sunday	3	4	5 Passover (begins at sundown)	6 ○ Full Moon	7 Good Friday (Western)	8
9 Easter (Western)	10 Easter Monday (Australia, Canada, Ireland, NZ, UK—except Scotland)	11	12	13 ◑ Last Quarter Passover ends	14 Holy Friday (Orthodox)	15
16 Easter (Orthodox)	17 Yom HaShoah (begins at sundown)	18	19	20 ● New Moon	21 Eid al-Fitr	22 Earth Day
23 St. George's Day (UK)	24	25 Anzac Day (NZ, Australia)	26	27 ◐ First Quarter	28	29
30						

MAY 2023

SUN	MON	TUE	WED	THU	FRi	SAT
	1 May Day (Australia—NT) Labour Day (Australia—QLD) Early May Bank Holiday (Ireland, UK)	2	3	4	5 ○ Full Moon	6
7	8	9	10	11	12 ◐ Last Quarter	13
14 Mother's Day (USA, Australia, Canada, NZ)	15	16	17	18	19 ● New Moon	20 Armed Forces Day (USA)
21	22 Victoria Day (Canada)	23	24	25	26	27 ◑ First Quarter
28	29 Memorial Day (USA) Bank Holiday (UK)	30	31			

JUNE 2023

SUN	MON	TUE	WED	THU	FRI	SAT
				1	2	3
4	5	6	7	8	9	10
O Full Moon	Queen's Birthday (NZ) Bank Holiday (Ireland)					◑ Last Quarter
11	12	13	14	15	16	17
	Queen's Birthday (Australia—except QLD, WA)		Flag Day (USA)			
18	19	20	21	22	23	24
● New Moon Father's Day (USA, Canada, Ireland, UK)	Juneteenth (USA)		Summer Solstice National Indigenous Peoples Day (Canada)			
25	26	27	28	29	30	
	◐ First Quarter		Eid al-Adha			

JULY 2023

SUN	MON	TUE	WED	THU	FRI	SAT
						1
						Canada Day
2	3	4	5	6	7	8
	○ Full Moon	Independence Day (USA)				
9	10	11	12	13	14	15
	◑ Last Quarter					
16	17	18	19	20	21	22
	● New Moon					
23	24	25	26	27	28	29
30	31					
	◐ First Quarter					

AuGUST 2023

SUN	MON	TUE	WED	THU	FRi	SAT
		1 ○ Full Moon	2	3	4	5
6	7 Bank Holiday (Ireland, UK—Scotland, Australia—NSW) Picnic Day (Australia—NT)	8 ◑ Last Quarter	9	10	11	12
13	14	15	16 ● New Moon	17	18	19
20	21	22	23	24 ◐ First Quarter	25	26
27	28 Bank Holiday (UK—except Scotland)	29	30	31 ○ Full Moon		

SePTeMBeR 2023

SUN	MON	TUE	WED	THU	FRI	SAT
					1	2
3 Father's Day (Australia, NZ)	4 Labor Day (USA, Canada)	5	6 ◑ Last Quarter	7	8	9
10	11	12	13	14	15 ● New Moon Rosh Hashanah (begins at sundown)	16
17 Rosh Hashanah ends	18	19	20	21 U.N. International Day of Peace	22 ◑ First Quarter	23 Autumnal Equinox
24 Yom Kippur (begins at sundown)	25 Queen's Birthday (Australia—WA)	26	27	28	29 ○ Full Moon	30

OCTOBER 2023

SUN	MON	TUE	WED	THU	FRI	SAT
1	2	3	4	5	6	7
	Labour Day (Australia—ACT, SA, NSW) Queen's Birthday (Australia—QLD)				◑ Last Quarter	
8	9	10	11	12	13	14
	Columbus Day (USA) Indigenous Peoples' Day (USA) Thanksgiving (Canada)					● New Moon
15	16	17	18	19	20	21
22	23	24	25	26	27	28
◐ First Quarter	Labour Day (NZ)	United Nations Day				○ Full Moon
29	30	31				
	Bank Holiday (Ireland)	Halloween				

November 2023

Sun	Mon	Tue	Wed	Thu	Fri	Sat
			1	2	3	4
5 ◐ Last Quarter Daylight Saving Time ends (USA, Canada)	6	7 Election Day (USA)	8	9	10	11 Veterans Day (USA) Remembrance Day (Canada, UK, Ireland, Australia)
12 Diwali Remembrance Sunday (UK, Ireland)	13 ● New Moon	14	15	16	17	18
19	20 ◑ First Quarter	21	22	23 Thanksgiving (USA)	24	25
26	27 ○ Full Moon	28	29	30 St. Andrew's Day (UK)		

DeCeMBeR 2023

SUN	MON	TUE	WED	THU	FRi	SAT
					1	2
3	4	5	6	7	8	9
		◑ Last Quarter		Hanukkah (begins at sundown)		
10	11	12	13	14	15	16
Human Rights Day		● New Moon			Hanukkah ends	
17	18	19	20	21	22	23
		◐ First Quarter			Winter Solstice	
24	25	26	27	28	29	30
Christmas Eve		Kwanzaa begins (USA) Boxing Day (Canada, NZ, UK, Australia—except SA) St. Stephen's Day (Ireland) Proclamation Day (Australia—SA)				
31	Christmas Day	○ Full Moon				

APPRECIATE the GOOD

I SEND the following BLESSINGS to OTHERS and TO the WORLD

I AM GRATEFUL for

LOVE MYSELF DEEPLY

I AM PROUD of MYSELF for

I AM LETTING GO of

MANIFEST and ATTRACT

I LISTEN DEEPLY then ASK CLEARLY for MY HEART'S DESIRES.
I AM MANIFESTING THIS or SOMETHING BETTER...

VISUALIZE iT

I CLOSE MY EYES for 3 MINUTES and IMAGINE HOW MY MANIFESTATION MIGHT TASTE, LOOK, FEEL, SMELL, and SOUND WHEN iT COMES TRUE.

TAKE INSPIRED ACTION

ONE ACTION I WILL TAKE in ALIGNMENT WITH MY DREAM is

WORD OR AFFIRMATION I WILL FOCUS ON to KEEP MY DREAMS ALIVE

AuG-SeP 2022

MONDAY
29
Bank Holiday (UK—except Scotland)

TUESDAY
30

WEDNESDAY
31

THURSDAY
1

FRIDAY
2

SATURDAY
3
◑ First Quarter

SUNDAY
4
Father's Day (Australia, NZ)

AUGUST 2022

S	M	T	W	T	F	S
	1	2	3	4	5	6
7	8	9	10	11	12	13
14	15	16	17	18	19	20
21	22	23	24	25	26	27
28	29	30	31			

SEPTEMBER 2022

S	M	T	W	T	F	S
				1	2	3
4	5	6	7	8	9	10
11	12	13	14	15	16	17
18	19	20	21	22	23	24
25	26	27	28	29	30	

APPRECIATE the GOOD

I SEND the FOLLOWING BLESSINGS to OTHERS
and TO the WORLD

I AM GRATEFUL for

LOVE MYSELF DEEPLY

I AM PROUD of MYSELF for

I AM LETTING GO of

MANIFEST and ATTRACT

I LISTEN DEEPLY then ASK CLEARLY for MY HEART'S DESIRES.
I AM MANIFESTING THIS or SOMETHING BETTER...

VISUALIZE IT

I CLOSE MY EYES for 3 MINUTES and
IMAGINE HOW MY MANIFESTATION MIGHT
TASTE, LOOK, FEEL, SMELL, and SOUND
WHEN IT COMES TRUE.

TAKE INSPIRED ACTION

ONE ACTION I WILL TAKE IN
ALIGNMENT WITH MY DREAM IS

WORD OR AFFIRMATION I WILL FOCUS ON to KEEP MY DREAMS ALIVE

SePTeMBeR 2022

MONDAY

5

Labor Day (USA, Canada)

TUESDAY

6

WEDNESDAY

7

THURSDAY

8

FRiDAY

9

SEPTEMBER 2022

S	M	T	W	T	F	S
				1	2	3
4	5	6	7	8	9	10
11	12	13	14	15	16	17
18	19	20	21	22	23	24
25	26	27	28	29	30	

SATURDAY

10

O Full Moon

OCTOBER 2022

S	M	T	W	T	F	S
						1
2	3	4	5	6	7	8
9	10	11	12	13	14	15
16	17	18	19	20	21	22
23	24	25	26	27	28	29
30	31					

SUNDAY

11

APPRECIATE the GOOD

I SEND the FOLLOWING BLESSINGS to OTHERS and TO the WORLD

I AM GRATEFUL for

LOVE MYSELF DEEPLY

I AM PROUD of MYSELF for

I AM LETTING GO of

MANIFEST and ATTRACT

I LISTEN DEEPLY then ASK CLEARLY for MY HEART'S DESIRES.
I AM MANIFESTING THIS or SOMETHING BETTER...

VISUALIZE IT

I CLOSE MY EYES for 3 MINUTES and IMAGINE HOW MY MANIFESTATION MIGHT TASTE, LOOK, FEEL, SMELL, and SOUND WHEN IT COMES TRUE.

TAKE INSPIRED ACTION

ONE ACTION I WILL TAKE in ALIGNMENT WITH MY DREAM is

WORD OR AFFIRMATION I WILL FOCUS ON to KEEP MY DREAMS ALIVE

SePTeMBeR 2022

MONDAY
12

TUESDAY
13

WEDNESDAY
14

THURSDAY
15

FRiDAY
16

SEPTEMBER 2022
S M T W T F S
          1 2 3
4 5 6 7 8 9 10
11 12 13 14 15 16 17
18 19 20 21 22 23 24
25 26 27 28 29 30

SATURDAY
17

◑ Last Quarter

OCTOBER 2022
S M T W T F S
                1
2 3 4 5 6 7 8
9 10 11 12 13 14 15
16 17 18 19 20 21 22
23 24 25 26 27 28 29
30 31

SUNDAY
18

APPRECIATE the GOOD

I SEND the following BLESSINGS to OTHERS
and To the WORLD

I AM GRATEFUL for

LOVE MYSELF DEEPLY

I AM PROUD of MYSELF for

I AM LETTING GO of

MANIFEST and ATTRACT

I LISTEN DEEPLY then ASK CLEARLY for MY HEART'S DESIRES.
I AM Manifesting THIS or SOMETHING BETTER...

VISUALIZE iT

I CLOSE MY EYES for 3 MINUTES and
IMAGINE HOW MY MANIFESTATION MIGHT
TASTE, LOOK, FEEL, SMELL, and SOUND
WHEN iT COMES TRUE.

TAKE INSPIRED ACTION

ONE ACTION I WILL TAKE in
ALIGNMENT WITH MY DREAM is

WORD OR AFFIRMATION I WILL FOCUS ON
to KEEP MY DREAMS ALIVE

September 2022

MONDAY
19

TUESDAY
20

WEDNESDAY
21

U.N. International Day of Peace

THURSDAY
22

FRIDAY
23

Autumnal Equinox

SATURDAY
24

SUNDAY
25

SEPTEMBER 2022
S	M	T	W	T	F	S
				1	2	3
4	5	6	7	8	9	10
11	12	13	14	15	16	17
18	19	20	21	22	23	24
25	26	27	28	29	30	

OCTOBER 2022
S	M	T	W	T	F	S
						1
2	3	4	5	6	7	8
9	10	11	12	13	14	15
16	17	18	19	20	21	22
23	24	25	26	27	28	29
30	31					

● New Moon • Rosh Hashanah (begins at sundown)

APPRECIATE the GOOD

I SEND the follOWING BLESSINGS to OTHERS and To the WORLD

I AM GRATEFUL for

LOVE MYSELF DEEPLY

I AM PROUD of MYSELF for

I AM LETTING GO of

MANiFeST and ATTRACT

I LISTEN DEEPLY then ASK CLEARLY for MY HEART'S DESIRES.
I AM MANifeSTING THIS or SOMETHING BETTER...

ViSUALIZE iT

I CLOSE MY EYES for 3 MiNuTES and IMAGINE HOW MY MANifeSTATION MiGHT TASTE, LOOK, FEEL, SMELL, and SOUND WHEN iT COMES TRUE.

TAKE INSPIRED ACTION

ONE ACTION I WILL TAKE in ALIGNMENT WITH MY DREAM is

WORD OR AFFIRMATION I WILL FOCUS ON to KEEP MY DREAMS ALIVE

MONDAY
26

Queen's Birthday (Australia—WA)

TUESDAY
27

Rosh Hashanah ends

WEDNESDAY
28

THURSDAY
29

FRIDAY
30

SEPTEMBER 2022

S	M	T	W	T	F	S
				1	2	3
4	5	6	7	8	9	10
11	12	13	14	15	16	17
18	19	20	21	22	23	24
25	26	27	28	29	30	

SATURDAY
1

OCTOBER 2022

S	M	T	W	T	F	S
						1
2	3	4	5	6	7	8
9	10	11	12	13	14	15
16	17	18	19	20	21	22
23	24	25	26	27	28	29
30	31					

SUNDAY
2

APPRECIATE the GOOD

I SEND the FOLLOWING BLESSINGS to OTHERS and TO the WORLD

I AM GRATEFUL for

LOVE MYSELF DEEPLY

I AM PROUD of MYSELF for

I AM LETTING GO of

MANIFEST and ATTRACT

I LISTEN DEEPLY then ASK CLEARLY for MY HEART'S DESIRES.
I AM MANIFESTING THIS or SOMETHING BETTER...

VISUALIZE IT

I CLOSE MY EYES for 3 MINUTES and IMAGINE HOW MY MANIFESTATION MIGHT TASTE, LOOK, FEEL, SMELL, and SOUND WHEN IT COMES TRUE.

TAKE INSPIRED ACTION

ONE ACTION I WILL TAKE in ALIGNMENT WITH MY DREAM is

WORD OR AFFIRMATION I WILL FOCUS ON to KEEP MY DREAMS ALIVE

OCTOBER 2022

MONDAY
3
◐ First Quarter
Labour Day (Australia—ACT, SA, NSW) • Queen's Birthday (Australia—QLD)

TUESDAY
4
Yom Kippur (begins at sundown)

WEDNESDAY
5

THURSDAY
6

FRIDAY
7

OCTOBER 2022						
S	M	T	W	T	F	S
						1
2	3	4	5	6	7	8
9	10	11	12	13	14	15
16	17	18	19	20	21	22
23	24	25	26	27	28	29
30	31					

SATURDAY
8

NOVEMBER 2022						
S	M	T	W	T	F	S
		1	2	3	4	5
6	7	8	9	10	11	12
13	14	15	16	17	18	19
20	21	22	23	24	25	26
27	28	29	30			

SUNDAY
9
○ Full Moon

APPRECIATE the GOOD

I SEND the fOllOWING BLESSINGS tO OTHERS
and TO the WORLD

I AM GRATEFUL fOr

LOVE MYSELF DEEPLY

I AM PROUD of MYSELF fOr

I AM LETTING GO of

MANIFESt and ATTRACT

I LISTEN DEEPLY then ASK CLEARLY fOr MY HEART'S DESIRES.
I AM MANIFESTING THIS Or SOMETHING BETTER...

VISUALIZE iT

I CLOSE MY EYES fOr 3 MINUTES and
IMAGINE HOW MY MANIFESTATION MIGHT
TASTE, LOOK, FEEL, SMELL, and SOUND
WHEN iT COMES TRUE.

TAKE INSPIRED ACTION

ONE ACTION I WILL TAKE in
ALIGNMENT WITH MY DREAM is

WORD OR AFFIRMATION I WILL FOCUS ON to KEEP MY DREAMS ALIVE

OCTOBeR 2022

MONDAY
10

Columbus Day (USA) • Indigenous Peoples' Day (USA) • Thanksgiving (Canada)

TUESDAY
11

WEDNESDAY
12

THURSDAY
13

FRiDAY
14

OCTOBER 2022
S	M	T	W	T	F	S
						1
2	3	4	5	6	7	8
9	10	11	12	13	14	15
16	17	18	19	20	21	22
23	24	25	26	27	28	29
30	31					

SATURDAY
15

NOVEMBER 2022
S	M	T	W	T	F	S
		1	2	3	4	5
6	7	8	9	10	11	12
13	14	15	16	17	18	19
20	21	22	23	24	25	26
27	28	29	30			

SUNDAY
16

APPRECIATE the GOOD

I SEND the fOllOWING BLESSINGS to OTHeRS
and TO the WORLD

I AM GRATEful for

LOVE MYSelf DEEPLY

I AM PROUD of MYSelf for

I AM LETTING GO of

MANiFest and ATTRACT

I LISTEN DEEPLY then ASK CLEARLY for MY HEART'S DESiReS.
I AM MANifeSTING THiS or SOMETHING BeTTer...

ViSUALize iT

I CLOSE MY EYES for 3 MiNUTES and
IMAGiNE HOW MY MANiFeSTATION MiGHT
TASTE, LOOK, FeEL, SMELL, and SOUND
WHEN iT COMES TRUE.

TAKE INSPIReD ACTION

One ACTION I WILL TAKE iN
ALIGNMENT WITH MY DREAM iS

WORD OR AFFiRMATION I WILL FOCUS ON
to KEEP MY DREAMS ALIVE

OCTOBER 2022

MONDAY
17

◗ Last Quarter

TUESDAY
18

WEDNESDAY
19

THURSDAY
20

FRiDAY
21

SATURDAY
22

SUNDAY
23

OCTOBER 2022

S	M	T	W	T	F	S
						1
2	3	4	5	6	7	8
9	10	11	12	13	14	15
16	17	18	19	20	21	22
23	24	25	26	27	28	29
30	31					

NOVEMBER 2022

S	M	T	W	T	F	S
		1	2	3	4	5
6	7	8	9	10	11	12
13	14	15	16	17	18	19
20	21	22	23	24	25	26
27	28	29	30			

APPRECIATE the GOOD

I SEND the FOLLOWING BLESSINGS to OTHERS
and TO the WORLD

I AM GRATEFUL for

LOVE MYSELF DEEPLY

I AM PROUD of MYSELF for

I AM LETTING GO of

MANiFest and ATTRACT

I LISTEN DEEPLY then ASK CLEARLY for MY HEART'S DESiRES.
I AM MANiFESTiNG THiS or SOMETHING BETTER...

VISUALIZE iT

I CLOSE MY EYES for 3 MiNUTES and
IMAGiNE HOW MY MANiFESTATiON MiGHT
TASTE, LOOK, FEEL, SMELL, and SOUND
WHEN iT COMES TRUE.

TAKE INSPIRED ACTiON

ONE ACTiON I WiLL TAKE in
ALiGNMENT WiTH MY DREAM is

WORD OR AFFiRMATION I WiLL FOCUS ON
to
KEEP MY DREAMS ALiVE

OCTOBER 2022

MONDAY

24

Diwali • United Nations Day • Labour Day (NZ)

TUESDAY

25

● New Moon

WEDNESDAY

26

THURSDAY

27

FRIDAY

28

OCTOBER 2022

S	M	T	W	T	F	S
						1
2	3	4	5	6	7	8
9	10	11	12	13	14	15
16	17	18	19	20	21	22
23	24	25	26	27	28	29
30	31					

SATURDAY

29

NOVEMBER 2022

S	M	T	W	T	F	S
		1	2	3	4	5
6	7	8	9	10	11	12
13	14	15	16	17	18	19
20	21	22	23	24	25	26
27	28	29	30			

SUNDAY

30

APPRECIATE the GOOD

I SEND the fOLLOWING BLESSINGS to OTHeRS
and To the WORLD

I AM GRATEFUL for

LOVE MYSELF DEEPLY

I AM PROUD of MYSELF for

I AM LETTING GO of

MANiFest and ATTRACT

I LISTEN DEEPLY then ASK CLEARLY for MY HEART'S DeSiReS.
I AM MANIFESTING THiS or SOMETHING BeTTeR...

ViSUALiZe iT

I CLOSE MY EYES for 3 MINUTES and
IMAGINE HOW MY MANIFESTATION MIGHT
TASTE, LOOK, FeeL, SMELL, and SOUND
WHEN iT COMES TRUE.

TAKE INSPIRED ACTION

ONE ACTION I WILL TAKE in
ALIGNMENT WITH MY DReAM iS

WORD OR AFFIRMATION I WiLL FOCUS ON

to KEEP MY DREAMS ALiVE

OCT-NOV 2022

MONDAY
31
Halloween • Bank Holiday (Ireland)

TUESDAY
1
◐ First Quarter

WEDNESDAY
2

THURSDAY
3

FRIDAY
4

SATURDAY
5

SUNDAY
6
Daylight Saving Time ends (USA, Canada)

OCTOBER 2022

S	M	T	W	T	F	S
						1
2	3	4	5	6	7	8
9	10	11	12	13	14	15
16	17	18	19	20	21	22
23	24	25	26	27	28	29
30	31					

NOVEMBER 2022

S	M	T	W	T	F	S
		1	2	3	4	5
6	7	8	9	10	11	12
13	14	15	16	17	18	19
20	21	22	23	24	25	26
27	28	29	30			

APPRECIATE the GOOD

I SEND the fOLLOWING BLESSINGS to OTHERS
and TO the WORLD

I AM GRATEFUL for

LOVE MYSELF DEEPLY

I AM PROUD of MYSELF for

I AM LETTING GO of

MANIFEST and ATTRACT

I LISTEN DEEPLY then ASK CLEARLY for MY HEART'S DESIRES.
I AM MANIFESTING THIS or SOMETHING BETTER...

VISUALIZE IT

I CLOSE MY EYES for 3 MINUTES and
IMAGINE HOW MY MANIFESTATION MIGHT
TASTE, LOOK, FEEL, SMELL, and SOUND
WHEN IT COMES TRUE.

TAKE INSPIRED ACTION

ONE ACTION I WILL TAKE in
ALIGNMENT WITH MY DREAM is

WORD OR AFFIRMATION I WILL FOCUS ON to KEEP MY DREAMS ALIVE

November 2022

○ Full Moon
Election Day (USA)

Veterans Day (USA) • Remembrance Day (Canada, UK, Ireland, Australia)

NOVEMBER 2022

S	M	T	W	T	F	S
		1	2	3	4	5
6	7	8	9	10	11	12
13	14	15	16	17	18	19
20	21	22	23	24	25	26
27	28	29	30			

DECEMBER 2022

S	M	T	W	T	F	S
				1	2	3
4	5	6	7	8	9	10
11	12	13	14	15	16	17
18	19	20	21	22	23	24
25	26	27	28	29	30	31

Remembrance Sunday (UK, Ireland)

APPRECIATE the GOOD

I SEND the FOLLOWING BLESSINGS to OTHERS and TO the WORLD

I AM GRATEFUL for

LOVE MYSELF DEEPLY

I AM PROUD of MYSELF for

I AM LETTING GO of

MANIFEST and ATTRACT

I LISTEN DEEPLY then ASK CLEARLY for MY HEART'S DESIRES.
I AM MANIFESTING THIS or SOMETHING BETTER...

VISUALIZE IT

I CLOSE MY EYES for 3 MINUTES and IMAGINE HOW MY MANIFESTATION MIGHT TASTE, LOOK, FEEL, SMELL, and SOUND WHEN IT COMES TRUE.

TAKE INSPIRED ACTION

ONE ACTION I WILL TAKE in ALIGNMENT WITH MY DREAM is

WORD OR AFFIRMATION I WILL FOCUS ON to KEEP MY DREAMS ALIVE

November 2022

MONDAY
14

TUESDAY
15

WEDNESDAY
16

◑ Last Quarter

THURSDAY
17

FRIDAY
18

SATURDAY
19

NOVEMBER 2022						
S	M	T	W	T	F	S
		1	2	3	4	5
6	7	8	9	10	11	12
13	14	15	16	17	18	19
20	21	22	23	24	25	26
27	28	29	30			

SUNDAY
20

DECEMBER 2022						
S	M	T	W	T	F	S
				1	2	3
4	5	6	7	8	9	10
11	12	13	14	15	16	17
18	19	20	21	22	23	24
25	26	27	28	29	30	31

APPRECIATE the GOOD

I SEND the fOLLOWING BLESSINGS to OTHERS
and TO the WORLD

I AM GRATEFUL for

LOVE MYSELF DEEPLY

I AM PROUD of MYSELF for

I AM LETTING GO of

MANIFEST and ATTRACT

I LISTEN DEEPLY then ASK CLEARLY for MY HEART'S DESIRES.
I AM MANIFESTING THIS or SOMETHING BETTER...

VISUALIZE IT

I CLOSE MY EYES for 3 MINUTES and
IMAGINE HOW MY MANIFESTATION MIGHT
TASTE, LOOK, FEEL, SMELL, and SOUND
WHEN IT COMES TRUE.

TAKE INSPIRED ACTION

ONE ACTION I WILL TAKE in
ALIGNMENT WITH MY DREAM is

WORD OR AFFIRMATION I WILL FOCUS ON to KEEP MY DREAMS ALIVE

November 2022

MONDAY

21

TUESDAY

22

WEDNESDAY

23

● New Moon

THURSDAY

24

Thanksgiving (USA)

FRIDAY

25

NOVEMBER 2022

S	M	T	W	T	F	S
		1	2	3	4	5
6	7	8	9	10	11	12
13	14	15	16	17	18	19
20	21	22	23	24	25	26
27	28	29	30			

SATURDAY

26

DECEMBER 2022

S	M	T	W	T	F	S
				1	2	3
4	5	6	7	8	9	10
11	12	13	14	15	16	17
18	19	20	21	22	23	24
25	26	27	28	29	30	31

SUNDAY

27

APPRECIATE the GOOD

I SEND the fOllOWING BLESSINGS tO OTHERS
and TO the WORLD

I AM GRATEFUL for

LOVE MYSELF DEEPLY

I AM PROUD of MYSELF for

I AM LETTING GO of

MANIFEST and ATTRACT

I LISTEN DEEPLY then ASK CLEARLY for MY HEART'S DESIRES.
I AM MANIFESTING THIS or SOMETHING BETTER...

VISUALIZE IT

I CLOSE MY EYES for 3 MINUTES and
IMAGINE HOW MY MANIFESTATION MIGHT
TASTE, LOOK, FEEL, SMELL, and SOUND
WHEN IT COMES TRUE.

TAKE INSPIRED ACTION

ONE ACTION I WILL TAKE in
ALIGNMENT WITH MY DREAM is

WORD OR AFFIRMATION I WILL FOCUS ON
to KEEP MY DREAMS ALIVE

Nov-Dec 2022

MONDAY
28

TUESDAY
29

WEDNESDAY
30

◑ First Quarter
St. Andrew's Day (UK)

THURSDAY
1

FRIDAY
2

SATURDAY
3

SUNDAY
4

NOVEMBER 2022
S	M	T	W	T	F	S
		1	2	3	4	5
6	7	8	9	10	11	12
13	14	15	16	17	18	19
20	21	22	23	24	25	26
27	28	29	30			

DECEMBER 2022
S	M	T	W	T	F	S
				1	2	3
4	5	6	7	8	9	10
11	12	13	14	15	16	17
18	19	20	21	22	23	24
25	26	27	28	29	30	31

APPRECIATE the GOOD

I SEND the following BLESSINGS to OTHERS and To the WORLD

I AM GRATEFUL for

LOVE MYSELF DEEPLY

I AM PROUD of MYSELF for

I AM LETTING GO of

MANIFEST and ATTRACT

I LISTEN DEEPLY then ASK CLEARLY for MY HEART'S DESIRES.
I AM MANIFESTING THIS or SOMETHING BETTER...

VISUALIZE IT

I CLOSE MY EYES for 3 MINUTES and IMAGINE HOW MY MANIFESTATION MIGHT TASTE, LOOK, FEEL, SMELL, and SOUND WHEN IT COMES TRUE.

TAKE INSPIRED ACTION

ONE ACTION I WILL TAKE in ALIGNMENT WITH MY DREAM is

WORD OR AFFIRMATION I WILL FOCUS ON to KEEP MY DREAMS ALIVE

DeCeMBeR 2022

MONDAY
5

TUESDAY
6

WEDNESDAY
7

THURSDAY
8

O Full Moon

FRiDAY
9

SATURDAY
10

Human Rights Day

SUNDAY
11

DECEMBER 2022
S M T W T F S
            1 2 3
4 5 6 7 8 9 10
11 12 13 14 15 16 17
18 19 20 21 22 23 24
25 26 27 28 29 30 31

JANUARY 2023
S M T W T F S
1 2 3 4 5 6 7
8 9 10 11 12 13 14
15 16 17 18 19 20 21
22 23 24 25 26 27 28
29 30 31

APPRECIATE the GOOD

I SEND the FOLLOWING BLESSINGS to OTHERS and To the WORLD

I AM GRATEFUL for

LOVE MYSELF DEEPLY

I AM PROUD of MYSELF for

I AM LETTING GO of

MANIFEST and ATTRACT

I LISTEN DEEPLY then ASK CLEARLY for MY HEART'S DESIRES.
I AM MANIFESTING THIS or SOMETHING BETTER...

VISUALIZE IT

I CLOSE MY EYES for 3 MINUTES and IMAGINE HOW MY MANIFESTATION MIGHT TASTE, LOOK, FEEL, SMELL, and SOUND WHEN IT COMES TRUE.

TAKE INSPIRED ACTION

ONE ACTION I WILL TAKE in ALIGNMENT WITH MY DREAM is

WORD OR AFFIRMATION I WILL FOCUS ON to KEEP MY DREAMS ALIVE

DeCeMBeR 2022

TUESDAY

13

WEDNESDAY

14

THURSDAY

15

FRiDAY

16

◑ Last Quarter

DECEMBER 2022

S	M	T	W	T	F	S
				1	2	3
4	5	6	7	8	9	10
11	12	13	14	15	16	17
18	19	20	21	22	23	24
25	26	27	28	29	30	31

SATURDAY

17

JANUARY 2023

S	M	T	W	T	F	S
1	2	3	4	5	6	7
8	9	10	11	12	13	14
15	16	17	18	19	20	21
22	23	24	25	26	27	28
29	30	31				

SUNDAY

18

Hanukkah (begins at sundown)

APPRECIATE the GOOD

I SEND the following BLESSINGS to OTHERS and TO the WORLD

I AM GRATEFUL for

LOVE MYSELF DEEPLY

I AM PROUD of MYSELF for

I AM LETTING GO of

MANIFEST and ATTRACT

I LISTEN DEEPLY then ASK CLEARLY for MY HEART'S DESIRES. I AM MANIFESTING THIS or SOMETHING BETTER...

VISUALIZE IT

I CLOSE MY EYES for 3 MINUTES and IMAGINE HOW MY MANIFESTATION MIGHT TASTE, LOOK, FEEL, SMELL, and SOUND WHEN IT COMES TRUE.

TAKE INSPIRED ACTION

ONE ACTION I WILL TAKE in ALIGNMENT WITH MY DREAM is

WORD OR AFFIRMATION I WILL FOCUS ON to KEEP MY DREAMS ALIVE

DeCeMBeR 2022

MONDAY

19

TUESDAY

20

WEDNESDAY

21

Winter Solstice

THURSDAY

22

FRiDAY

23

● New Moon

SATURDAY

24

Christmas Eve

SUNDAY

25

Christmas Day

DECEMBER 2022

S	M	T	W	T	F	S
				1	2	3
4	5	6	7	8	9	10
11	12	13	14	15	16	17
18	19	20	21	22	23	24
25	26	27	28	29	30	31

JANUARY 2023

S	M	T	W	T	F	S
1	2	3	4	5	6	7
8	9	10	11	12	13	14
15	16	17	18	19	20	21
22	23	24	25	26	27	28
29	30	31				

APPRECIATE the GOOD

I SEND the fOllOWING BLESSINGS to OTHERS
and TO the WORLD

I AM GRATEFUL for

LOVE myself DEEPLY

I AM PROUD of MYSELF for

I AM LETTING GO of

MANifest and ATTRACT

I LISTEN DEEPLY then ASK CLEARLY for MY HEART'S DESIRES.
I AM MANifesting THIS or SOMETHING BETTER...

ViSUALize iT

I CLOSE MY EYES for 3 MINUTES and
IMAGINE HOW MY MANIFESTATION MIGHT
TASTE, LOOK, FEEL, SMELL, and SOUND
WHEN iT COMES TRUE.

TAKE INSPIRED ACTION

ONE ACTION I WILL TAKE IN
ALIGNMENT WITH MY DREAM iS

WORD OR AFFiRMATiON I WiLL FOCUS ON
to KEEP MY DREAMS ALiVE

Dec 2022 - Jan 2023

MONDAY
26

Kwanzaa begins (USA) • Hanukkah ends • Christmas Day (observed) (Australia—NT, SA, WA)
Boxing Day (Canada, NZ, UK, Australia—except NT, SA, WA) • St. Stephen's Day (Ireland)

TUESDAY
27

Christmas Day (observed) (NZ, UK, Australia—except NT, SA, WA)
Boxing Day (observed) (Australia—NT, WA) • Proclamation Day (observed) (Australia—SA)

WEDNESDAY
28

THURSDAY
29

FRIDAY
30

◑ First Quarter

SATURDAY
31

DECEMBER 2022

S	M	T	W	T	F	S
				1	2	3
4	5	6	7	8	9	10
11	12	13	14	15	16	17
18	19	20	21	22	23	24
25	26	27	28	29	30	31

SUNDAY
1

JANUARY 2023

S	M	T	W	T	F	S
1	2	3	4	5	6	7
8	9	10	11	12	13	14
15	16	17	18	19	20	21
22	23	24	25	26	27	28
29	30	31				

New Year's Day • Kwanzaa ends (USA)

APPRECIATE the GOOD

I SEND the following BLESSINGS to OTHERS
and TO the WORLD

I AM GRATEFUL for

LOVE MYSELF DEEPLY

I AM PROUD of MYSELF for

I AM LETTING GO of

MANIFEST and ATTRACT

I LISTEN DEEPLY then ASK CLEARLY for MY HEART'S DESIRES.
I AM MANIFESTING THIS or SOMETHING BETTER...

VISUALIZE IT

I CLOSE MY EYES for 3 MINUTES and
IMAGINE HOW MY MANIFESTATION MIGHT
TASTE, LOOK, FEEL, SMELL, and SOUND
WHEN IT COMES TRUE.

TAKE INSPIRED ACTION

ONE ACTION I WILL TAKE IN
ALIGNMENT WITH MY DREAM IS

WORD OR AFFIRMATION I WILL FOCUS ON to KEEP MY DREAMS ALIVE

JaNuaRY 2023

MONDAY

2

New Year's Day (observed) (NZ, Australia, UK)

TUESDAY

3

Bank Holiday (UK—Scotland)

WEDNESDAY

4

THURSDAY

5

FRiDAY

6

○ Full Moon

SATURDAY

7

SUNDAY

8

JANUARY 2023

S	M	T	W	T	F	S
1	2	3	4	5	6	7
8	9	10	11	12	13	14
15	16	17	18	19	20	21
22	23	24	25	26	27	28
29	30	31				

FEBRUARY 2023

S	M	T	W	T	F	S
			1	2	3	4
5	6	7	8	9	10	11
12	13	14	15	16	17	18
19	20	21	22	23	24	25
26	27	28				

APPRECIATE the GOOD

I SEND the FOLLOWING BLESSINGS to OTHERS
and TO the WORLD

I AM GRATEFUL for

LOVE MYSELF DEEPLY

I AM PROUD of MYSELF for

I AM LETTING GO of

MANIFEST and ATTRACT

I LISTEN DEEPLY then ASK CLEARLY for MY HEART'S DESIRES.
I AM MANIFESTING THIS or SOMETHING BETTER...

VISUALIZE IT

I CLOSE MY EYES for 3 MINUTES and
IMAGINE HOW MY MANIFESTATION MIGHT
TASTE, LOOK, FEEL, SMELL, and SOUND
WHEN IT COMES TRUE.

TAKE INSPIRED ACTION

ONE ACTION I WILL TAKE in
ALIGNMENT WITH MY DREAM IS

WORD OR AFFIRMATION I WILL FOCUS ON
to KEEP MY DREAMS ALIVE

JANUARY 2023

MONDAY
9

TUESDAY
10

WEDNESDAY
11

THURSDAY
12

FRIDAY
13

SATURDAY
14

SUNDAY
15

JANUARY 2023
S M T W T F S
1 2 3 4 5 6 7
8 9 10 11 12 13 14
15 16 17 18 19 20 21
22 23 24 25 26 27 28
29 30 31

FEBRUARY 2023
S M T W T F S
1 2 3 4
5 6 7 8 9 10 11
12 13 14 15 16 17 18
19 20 21 22 23 24 25
26 27 28

◑ Last Quarter

APPRECIATE the GOOD

I SEND the fOLLOWING BLESSINGS to OTHERS and To the WORLD

I AM GRATEFUL for

LOVE MYSELF DEEPLY

I AM PROUD of MYSELF for

I AM LETTING GO of

MANIFEST and ATTRACT

I LISTEN DEEPLY then ASK CLEARLY for MY HEART'S DESIRES.
I AM MANIFESTING THIS or SOMETHING BETTER...

VISUALIZE IT

I CLOSE MY EYES for 3 MINUTES and IMAGINE HOW MY MANIFESTATION MIGHT TASTE, LOOK, FEEL, SMELL, and SOUND WHEN IT COMES TRUE.

TAKE INSPIRED ACTION

ONE ACTION I WILL TAKE in ALIGNMENT WITH MY DREAM is

WORD OR AFFIRMATION I WILL FOCUS ON to KEEP MY DREAMS ALIVE

JaNuaRY 2023

MONDAY
16
Martin Luther King Jr. Day (USA)

TUESDAY
17

WEDNESDAY
18

THURSDAY
19

FRiDAY
20

SATURDAY
21
● New Moon

SUNDAY
22
Lunar New Year (Year of the Rabbit)

JANUARY 2023
S	M	T	W	T	F	S
1	2	3	4	5	6	7
8	9	10	11	12	13	14
15	16	17	18	19	20	21
22	23	24	25	26	27	28
29	30	31				

FEBRUARY 2023
S	M	T	W	T	F	S
			1	2	3	4
5	6	7	8	9	10	11
12	13	14	15	16	17	18
19	20	21	22	23	24	25
26	27	28				

APPRECIATE the GOOD

I SEND the FOLLOWING BLESSINGS to OTHERS and TO the WORLD

I AM GRATEFUL for

LOVE MYSELF DEEPLY

I AM PROUD of MYSELF for

I AM LETTING GO of

MANIFEST and ATTRACT

I LISTEN DEEPLY then ASK CLEARLY for MY HEART'S DESIRES.
I AM MANIFESTING THIS or SOMETHING BETTER...

VISUALIZE IT

I CLOSE MY EYES for 3 MINUTES and IMAGINE HOW MY MANIFESTATION MIGHT TASTE, LOOK, FEEL, SMELL, and SOUND WHEN IT COMES TRUE.

TAKE INSPIRED ACTION

ONE ACTION I WILL TAKE in ALIGNMENT WITH MY DREAM IS

WORD OR AFFIRMATION I WILL FOCUS ON to KEEP MY DREAMS ALIVE

JaNuaRY 2023

MONDAY
23

TUESDAY
24

WEDNESDAY
25

THURSDAY
26

Australia Day

FRiDAY
27

JANUARY 2023
S M T W T F S
1 2 3 4 5 6 7
8 9 10 11 12 13 14
15 16 17 18 19 20 21
22 23 24 25 26 27 28
29 30 31

SATURDAY
28

◑ First Quarter

SUNDAY
29

FEBRUARY 2023
S M T W T F S
1 2 3 4
5 6 7 8 9 10 11
12 13 14 15 16 17 18
19 20 21 22 23 24 25
26 27 28

APPRECIATE the GOOD

I SEND the fOLLOWING BLESSINGS to OTHERS
and To the WORLD

I AM GRATEFUL for

LOVE MYSELF DEEPLY

I AM PROUD of MYSELF for

I AM LETTING GO of

MANIFEST and ATTRACT

I LISTEN DEEPLY then ASK CLEARLY for MY HEART'S DESIRES.
I AM MANIFESTING THIS or SOMETHING BETTER...

VISUALIZE IT

I CLOSE MY EYES for 3 MINUTES and
IMAGINE HOW MY MANIFESTATION MIGHT
TASTE, LOOK, FEEL, SMELL, and SOUND
WHEN IT COMES TRUE.

TAKE INSPIRED ACTION

One ACTION I WILL TAKE in
ALIGNMENT WITH MY DREAM is

WORD OR AFFIRMATION I WILL FOCUS ON to KEEP MY DREAMS ALIVE

Jan-Feb 2023

MONDAY
30

TUESDAY
31

WEDNESDAY
1

THURSDAY
2

FRIDAY
3

SATURDAY
4

SUNDAY
5

○ Full Moon

JANUARY 2023

S	M	T	W	T	F	S
1	2	3	4	5	6	7
8	9	10	11	12	13	14
15	16	17	18	19	20	21
22	23	24	25	26	27	28
29	30	31				

FEBRUARY 2023

S	M	T	W	T	F	S
			1	2	3	4
5	6	7	8	9	10	11
12	13	14	15	16	17	18
19	20	21	22	23	24	25
26	27	28				

APPRECIATE the GOOD

I SEND the following BLESSINGS to OTHERS and TO the WORLD

I AM GRATEFUL for

LOVE MYSELF DEEPLY

I AM PROUD of MYSELF for

I AM LETTING GO of

MANIFEST and ATTRACT

I LISTEN DEEPLY then ASK CLEARLY for MY HEART'S DESIRES.
I AM MANIFESTING THIS or SOMETHING BETTER...

VISUALIZE iT

I CLOSE MY EYES for 3 MINUTES and IMAGINE HOW MY MANIFESTATION MIGHT TASTE, LOOK, FEEL, SMELL, and SOUND WHEN iT COMES TRUE.

TAKE INSPIRED ACTION

ONE ACTION I WILL TAKE in ALIGNMENT WITH MY DREAM is

WORD OR AFFIRMATION I WILL FOCUS ON to KEEP MY DREAMS ALIVE

FeBRuaRY 2023

MONDAY
6
Waitangi Day (NZ)

TUESDAY
7

WEDNESDAY
8

THURSDAY
9

FRiDAY
10

SATURDAY
11

SUNDAY
12

FEBRUARY 2023

S	M	T	W	T	F	S
			1	2	3	4
5	6	7	8	9	10	11
12	13	14	15	16	17	18
19	20	21	22	23	24	25
26	27	28				

MARCH 2023

S	M	T	W	T	F	S
			1	2	3	4
5	6	7	8	9	10	11
12	13	14	15	16	17	18
19	20	21	22	23	24	25
26	27	28	29	30	31	

APPRECIATE the GOOD

I SEND the following BLESSINGS to OTHERS
and TO the WORLD

I AM GRATEFUL for

LOVE MYSELF DEEPLY

I AM PROUD of MYSELF for

I AM LETTING GO of

MANIFEST and ATTRACT

I LISTEN DEEPLY then ASK CLEARLY for MY HEART'S DESIRES.
I AM MANIFESTING THIS or SOMETHING BETTER...

VISUALIZE iT

I CLOSE MY EYES for 3 MINUTES and
IMAGINE HOW MY MANIFESTATION MIGHT
TASTE, LOOK, FEEL, SMELL, and SOUND
WHEN iT COMES TRUE.

TAKE INSPIRED ACTION

ONE ACTION I WILL TAKE in
ALIGNMENT WITH MY DREAM is

WORD OR AFFIRMATION I WILL FOCUS ON to KEEP MY DREAMS ALIVE

FeBRUaRY 2023

MONDAY

13

◑ Last Quarter

TUESDAY

14

St. Valentine's Day

WEDNESDAY

15

THURSDAY

16

FRiDAY

17

SATURDAY

18

SUNDAY

19

FEBRUARY 2023

S	M	T	W	T	F	S
			1	2	3	4
5	6	7	8	9	10	11
12	13	14	15	16	17	18
19	20	21	22	23	24	25
26	27	28				

MARCH 2023

S	M	T	W	T	F	S
			1	2	3	4
5	6	7	8	9	10	11
12	13	14	15	16	17	18
19	20	21	22	23	24	25
26	27	28	29	30	31	

APPRECIATE the GOOD

I SEND the fOLLOWiNG BLESSiNGS to OTHeRS
and To the WORLD

I AM GRATEFUL for

LOVE MYSELF DEEPLY

I AM PROUD of MYSELF for

I AM LETTiNG GO of

MANiFeST and ATTRACT

I LiSTEN DEEPLY then ASK CLEARLY for MY HEART'S DeSiReS.
I AM ManiFesTiNG THiS or SOMETHiNG BeTTER...

ViSUALiZE iT

I CLOSE MY EYES for 3 MiNUTES and
IMAGiNE HOW MY MANiFeSTATiON MiGHT
TASTE, LOOK, FeeL, SMELL, and SOUND
WHEN iT COMES TRUE.

TAKE INSPiReD ACTiON

ONE ACTiON I WiLL TAKE in
ALiGNMENT WiTH MY DREAM is

WORD OR AFFiRMATiON I WiLL FOCUS ON
to KEEP MY DREAMS ALiVE

FeBRuaRY 2023

MONDAY
20
● New Moon
Presidents' Day (USA)

TUESDAY
21

WEDNESDAY
22

Ash Wednesday

THURSDAY
23

FRiDAY
24

SATURDAY
25

SUNDAY
26

FEBRUARY 2023

S	M	T	W	T	F	S
			1	2	3	4
5	6	7	8	9	10	11
12	13	14	15	16	17	18
19	20	21	22	23	24	25
26	27	28				

MARCH 2023

S	M	T	W	T	F	S
			1	2	3	4
5	6	7	8	9	10	11
12	13	14	15	16	17	18
19	20	21	22	23	24	25
26	27	28	29	30	31	

APPRECIATE the GOOD

I SEND the following BLESSINGS to OTHERS
and TO the WORLD

I AM GRATEFUL for

LOVE myself DEEPLY

I AM PROUD of MYSELF for

I AM LETTING GO of

MANIFEST and ATTRACT

I LISTEN DEEPLY then ASK CLEARLY for MY HEART'S DESIRES.
I AM MANIFESTING THIS or SOMETHING BETTER...

VISUALIZE IT

I CLOSE MY EYES for 3 MINUTES and
IMAGINE HOW MY MANIFESTATION MIGHT
TASTE, LOOK, FEEL, SMELL, and SOUND
WHEN IT COMES TRUE.

TAKE INSPIRED ACTION

ONE ACTION I WILL TAKE in
ALIGNMENT WITH MY DREAM is

WORD OR AFFIRMATION I WILL FOCUS ON
to KEEP MY DREAMS ALIVE

FeB-MaR 2023

MONDAY

27

◖ First Quarter

TUESDAY

28

WEDNESDAY

1

St. David's Day (UK)

THURSDAY

2

FRiDAY

3

FEBRUARY 2023

S	M	T	W	T	F	S
			1	2	3	4
5	6	7	8	9	10	11
12	13	14	15	16	17	18
19	20	21	22	23	24	25
26	27	28				

SATURDAY

4

MARCH 2023

S	M	T	W	T	F	S
			1	2	3	4
5	6	7	8	9	10	11
12	13	14	15	16	17	18
19	20	21	22	23	24	25
26	27	28	29	30	31	

SUNDAY

5

APPRECIATE the GOOD

I SEND the FOLLOWING BLESSINGS to OTHERS
and TO the WORLD

I AM GRATEFUL for

LOVE myself DEEPLY

I AM PROUD of MYSELF for

I AM LETTING GO of

MANIFEST and ATTRACT

I LISTEN DEEPLY then ASK CLEARLY for MY HEART'S DESIRES.
I AM MANIFESTING THIS or SOMETHING BETTER...

VISUALIZE IT

I CLOSE MY EYES for 3 MINUTES and
IMAGINE HOW MY MANIFESTATION MIGHT
TASTE, LOOK, FEEL, SMELL, and SOUND
WHEN IT COMES TRUE.

TAKE INSPIRED ACTION

ONE ACTION I WILL TAKE IN
ALIGNMENT WITH MY DREAM IS

WORD OR AFFIRMATION I WILL FOCUS ON to KEEP MY DREAMS ALIVE

MaRCH 2023

6

Purim (begins at sundown) • Labour Day (Australia—WA)

7

O Full Moon

8

International Women's Day

9

10

MARCH 2023

S	M	T	W	T	F	S
			1	2	3	4
5	6	7	8	9	10	11
12	13	14	15	16	17	18
19	20	21	22	23	24	25
26	27	28	29	30	31	

11

APRIL 2023

S	M	T	W	T	F	S
						1
2	3	4	5	6	7	8
9	10	11	12	13	14	15
16	17	18	19	20	21	22
23	24	25	26	27	28	29
30						

12

Daylight Saving Time begins (USA, Canada)

APPRECIATE the GOOD

I SEND the following BLESSINGS to OTHERS
and TO the WORLD

I AM GRATEFUL for

LOVE MYSELF DEEPLY

I AM PROUD of MYSELF for

I AM LETTING GO of

MANiFest and ATTRACT

I LISTEN DEEPLY then ASK CLEARLY for MY HEART'S DESiRES.
I AM MANifesting THIS or SOMETHING BETTER...

VISUALiZE iT

I CLOSE MY EYES for 3 MiNUTES and
IMAGiNE HOW MY MANiFESTATiON MiGHT
TASTE, LOOK, FEEL, SMELL, and SOUND
WHEN iT COMES TRUE.

TAKE INSPIRED ACTiON

ONE ACTION I WiLL TAKE iN
ALIGNMENT WiTH MY DREAM iS

WORD OR AFFiRMATiON I WiLL FOCUS ON
to KEEP MY DREAMS ALiVE

MaRCH 2023

MONDAY
13
Eight Hours Day (Australia—TAS) • Labour Day (Australia—VIC) • Commonwealth Day (Australia, Canada, NZ, UK)

TUESDAY
14

WEDNESDAY
15
◑ Last Quarter

THURSDAY
16

FRIDAY
17
St. Patrick's Day

SATURDAY
18

MARCH 2023						
S	M	T	W	T	F	S
			1	2	3	4
5	6	7	8	9	10	11
12	13	14	15	16	17	18
19	20	21	22	23	24	25
26	27	28	29	30	31	

SUNDAY
19
Mothering Sunday (Ireland, UK)

APRIL 2023						
S	M	T	W	T	F	S
						1
2	3	4	5	6	7	8
9	10	11	12	13	14	15
16	17	18	19	20	21	22
23	24	25	26	27	28	29
30						

APPRECIATE the GOOD

I SEND the following BLESSINGS to OTHERS and TO the WORLD

I AM GRATEFUL for

LOVE MYSELF DEEPLY

I AM PROUD of MYSELF for

I AM LETTING GO of

MANiFest and ATTRACT

I LISTEN DEEPLY then ASK CLEARLY for MY HEART'S DESiRES.
I AM Manifesting THiS or SOMETHING BETTER...

VISUALIZE iT

I CLOSE MY EYES for 3 MiNUTES and
IMAGiNE HOW MY MANiFESTATiON MiGHT
TASTE, LOOK, FEEL, SMELL, and SOUND
WHEN iT COMES TRUE.

TAKE iNSPiRED ACTiON

One ACTiON I WiLL TAKE in
ALiGNMENT WiTH MY DREAM is

WORD OR AFFiRMATiON I WiLL FOCUS ON
to KEEP MY DREAMS ALiVE

MaRCH 2023

MONDAY

20

Vernal Equinox

TUESDAY

21

● New Moon

WEDNESDAY

22

Ramadan

THURSDAY

23

FRiDAY

24

SATURDAY

25

SUNDAY

26

MARCH 2023

S	M	T	W	T	F	S
			1	2	3	4
5	6	7	8	9	10	11
12	13	14	15	16	17	18
19	20	21	22	23	24	25
26	27	28	29	30	31	

APRIL 2023

S	M	T	W	T	F	S
						1
2	3	4	5	6	7	8
9	10	11	12	13	14	15
16	17	18	19	20	21	22
23	24	25	26	27	28	29
30						

APPRECIATE the GOOD

I SEND the following BLESSINGS to OTHERS and TO the WORLD

I AM GRATEFUL for

LOVE MYSELF DEEPLY

I AM PROUD of MYSELF for

I AM LETTING GO of

MANiFEST and ATTRACT

I LISTEN DEEPLY then ASK CLEARLY for MY HEART'S DESiRES.
I AM MANiFESTiNG THIS or SOMETHiNG BETTER...

VISUALIZE iT

I CLOSE MY EYES for 3 MiNUTES and IMAGINE HOW MY MANiFESTATION MiGHT TASTE, LOOK, FEEL, SMELL, and SOUND WHEN iT COMES TRUE.

TAKE INSPIRED ACTION

ONE ACTION I WILL TAKE iN ALIGNMENT WiTH MY DREAM is

WORD OR AFFIRMATION I WILL FOCUS ON to KEEP MY DREAMS ALIVE

MaR-APR 2023

MONDAY
27

TUESDAY
28

WEDNESDAY
29

◑ First Quarter

THURSDAY
30

FRIDAY
31

SATURDAY
1

MARCH 2023

S	M	T	W	T	F	S
			1	2	3	4
5	6	7	8	9	10	11
12	13	14	15	16	17	18
19	20	21	22	23	24	25
26	27	28	29	30	31	

SUNDAY
2

APRIL 2023

S	M	T	W	T	F	S
						1
2	3	4	5	6	7	8
9	10	11	12	13	14	15
16	17	18	19	20	21	22
23	24	25	26	27	28	29
30						

Palm Sunday

APPRECIATE the GOOD

I SEND the fOLLOWING BLESSINGS to OTHERS and TO the WORLD

I AM GRATEFUL for

LOVE MYSELF DEEPLY

I AM PROUD of MYSELF for

I AM LETTING GO of

MANIFEST and ATTRACT

I LISTEN DEEPLY then ASK CLEARLY for MY HEART'S DESIRES.
I AM MANIFESTING THIS or SOMETHING BETTER...

VISUALIZE IT

I CLOSE MY EYES for 3 MINUTES and IMAGINE HOW MY MANIFESTATION MIGHT TASTE, LOOK, FEEL, SMELL, and SOUND WHEN IT COMES TRUE.

TAKE INSPIRED ACTION

One ACTION I WILL TAKE in ALIGNMENT WITH MY DREAM is

WORD OR AFFIRMATION I WILL FOCUS ON to KEEP MY DREAMS ALIVE

APRiL 2023

MONDAY
3

TUESDAY
4

WEDNESDAY
5

Passover (begins at sundown)

THURSDAY
6

O Full Moon

FRiDAY
7

Good Friday (Western)

APRIL 2023
S M T W T F S
                1
2 3 4 5 6 7 8
9 10 11 12 13 14 15
16 17 18 19 20 21 22
23 24 25 26 27 28 29
30

SATURDAY
8

MAY 2023
S M T W T F S
    1 2 3 4 5 6
7 8 9 10 11 12 13
14 15 16 17 18 19 20
21 22 23 24 25 26 27
28 29 30 31

SUNDAY
9

Easter (Western)

APPRECIATE the GOOD

I SEND the FOLLOWING BLESSINGS to OTHERS and to the WORLD

I AM GRATEFUL for

LOVE MYSELF DEEPLY

I AM PROUD of MYSELF for

I AM LETTING GO of

MANIFEST and ATTRACT

I LISTEN DEEPLY then ASK CLEARLY for MY HEART'S DESIRES.
I AM MANIFESTING THIS or SOMETHING BETTER...

VISUALIZE IT

I CLOSE MY EYES for 3 MINUTES and IMAGINE HOW MY MANIFESTATION MIGHT TASTE, LOOK, FEEL, SMELL, and SOUND WHEN IT COMES TRUE.

TAKE INSPIRED ACTION

ONE ACTION I WILL TAKE in ALIGNMENT WITH MY DREAM is

WORD OR AFFIRMATION I WILL FOCUS ON to KEEP MY DREAMS ALIVE

APRIL 2023

MONDAY
10
Easter Monday (Australia, Canada, Ireland, NZ, UK—except Scotland)

TUESDAY
11

WEDNESDAY
12

THURSDAY
13
◑ Last Quarter
Passover ends

FRIDAY
14
Holy Friday (Orthodox)

SATURDAY
15

SUNDAY
16
Easter (Orthodox)

APPRECIATE the GOOD

I SEND the fOLLOWING BLESSINGS to OTHERS and TO the WORLD

I AM GRATEFUL for

LOVE MYSELF DEEPLY

I AM PROUD of MYSELF for

I AM LETTING GO of

MANIFEST and ATTRACT

I LISTEN DEEPLY then ASK CLEARLY for MY HEART'S DESiRES.
I AM MANiFesTiNG THIS or SOMETHING BETTER...

VISUALIZE iT

I CLOSE MY EYES for 3 MiNUTES and IMAGINE HOW MY MANiFESTATiON MiGHT TASTE, LOOK, FEEL, SMELL, and SOUND WHEN iT COMES TRUE.

TAKE INSPiRED ACTiON

ONE ACTiON I WiLL TAKE iN ALiGNMENT WiTH MY DREAM is

WORD OR AFFiRMATiON I WiLL FOCUS ON to KEEP MY DREAMS ALiVE

APRIL 2023

MONDAY
17

Yom HaShoah (begins at sundown)

TUESDAY
18

WEDNESDAY
19

THURSDAY
20

● New Moon

FRIDAY
21

Eid al-Fitr

APRIL 2023
S M T W T F S
              1
2 3 4 5 6 7 8
9 10 11 12 13 14 15
16 17 18 19 20 21 22
23 24 25 26 27 28 29
30

SATURDAY
22

Earth Day

MAY 2023
S M T W T F S
    1 2 3 4 5 6
7 8 9 10 11 12 13
14 15 16 17 18 19 20
21 22 23 24 25 26 27
28 29 30 31

SUNDAY
23

St. George's Day (UK)

APPRECIATE the GOOD

I SEND the following BLESSINGS to OTHERS and TO the WORLD

I AM GRATEFUL for

LOVE MYSELF DEEPLY

I AM PROUD of MYSELF for

I AM LETTING GO of

MANIFEST and ATTRACT

I LISTEN DEEPLY then ASK CLEARLY for MY HEART'S DESIRES.
I AM MANIFESTING THIS or SOMETHING BETTER...

VISUALIZE IT

I CLOSE MY EYES for 3 MINUTES and IMAGINE HOW MY MANIFESTATION MIGHT TASTE, LOOK, FEEL, SMELL, and SOUND WHEN IT COMES TRUE.

TAKE INSPIRED ACTION

ONE ACTION I WILL TAKE in ALIGNMENT WITH MY DREAM is

WORD OR AFFIRMATION I WILL FOCUS ON to KEEP MY DREAMS ALIVE

APRIL 2023

MONDAY

24

TUESDAY

25

Anzac Day (NZ, Australia)

WEDNESDAY

26

THURSDAY

27

◐ First Quarter

FRIDAY

28

APRIL 2023

S	M	T	W	T	F	S
						1
2	3	4	5	6	7	8
9	10	11	12	13	14	15
16	17	18	19	20	21	22
23	24	25	26	27	28	29
30						

SATURDAY

29

MAY 2023

S	M	T	W	T	F	S
	1	2	3	4	5	6
7	8	9	10	11	12	13
14	15	16	17	18	19	20
21	22	23	24	25	26	27
28	29	30	31			

SUNDAY

30

APPRECIATE the GOOD

I SEND the following BLESSINGS to OTHERS
and To the WORLD

I AM GRATEFUL for

LOVE MYSELF DEEPLY

I AM PROUD of MYSELF for

I AM LETTING GO of

MANIFEST and ATTRACT

I LISTEN DEEPLY then ASK CLEARLY for MY HEART'S DESIRES.
I AM Manifesting THIS or SOMETHING BETTER...

VISUALIZE iT

I CLOSE MY EYES for 3 MINUTES and
IMAGINE HOW MY MANIFESTATION MIGHT
TASTE, LOOK, FEEL, SMELL, and SOUND
WHEN iT COMES TRUE.

TAKE INSPIRED ACTION

One ACTION I WILL TAKE in
ALIGNMENT WITH MY DREAM is

WORD OR AFFIRMATION I WILL FOCUS ON to KEEP MY DREAMS ALIVE

MAY 2023

MONDAY
1

May Day (Australia—NT) • Labour Day (Australia—QLD) • Early May Bank Holiday (Ireland, UK)

TUESDAY
2

WEDNESDAY
3

THURSDAY
4

FRIDAY
5

○ Full Moon

SATURDAY
6

SUNDAY
7

APPRECIATE the GOOD

I SEND the fOllOWING BLESSINGS to OTHERS
and To the WORLD

I AM GRATEFUL for

LOVE MYSelf DEEPLY

I AM PROUD of MYSelf for

I AM LETTING GO of

MANiFest and ATTRACT

I LISTEN DEEPLY then ASK CLEARLY for MY HEART'S DESiReS.
I AM MAniFesting THiS or SOMETHING BETTER...

ViSUALiZe iT

I CLOSE MY EYES for 3 MiNuTES and
IMAGiNe HOW MY MANiFeStATiON MiGHT
TASTE, LOOK, FEEL, SMELL, and SOUND
WHEN iT COMES TRUE.

TAKE INSPiReD ACTiON

One ACTiON I WiLL TAKE in
ALiGNMENT WiTH MY DREAM is

WORD OR AFFiRMATiON I WiLL FOCUS ON to KEEP MY DREAMS ALiVE

MAY 2023

MONDAY
8

TUESDAY
9

WEDNESDAY
10

THURSDAY
11

FRIDAY
12

◑ Last Quarter

SATURDAY
13

SUNDAY
14

Mother's Day (USA, Australia, Canada, NZ)

MAY 2023

S	M	T	W	T	F	S
	1	2	3	4	5	6
7	8	9	10	11	12	13
14	15	16	17	18	19	20
21	22	23	24	25	26	27
28	29	30	31			

JUNE 2023

S	M	T	W	T	F	S
				1	2	3
4	5	6	7	8	9	10
11	12	13	14	15	16	17
18	19	20	21	22	23	24
25	26	27	28	29	30	

APPRECIATE the GOOD

I SEND the fOLLOWING BLESSINGS to OTHERS and TO the WORLD

I AM GRATEFUL for

LOVE MYSELF DEEPLY

I AM PROUD of MYSELF for

I AM LETTING GO of

MANiFest and ATTRACT

I LISTEN DEEPLY then ASK CLEARLY for MY HEART'S DESiRES.
I AM MANiFesting THis or SOMETHING BETTER...

ViSUALiZE iT

I CLOSE MY EYES for 3 MiNUTES and IMAGiNE HOW MY MANiFESTATION MiGHT TASTE, LOOK, FEEL, SMELL, and SOUND WHEN iT COMES TRUE.

TAKE iNSPiRED ACTiON

One ACTiON I WiLL TAKE in ALiGNMENT WiTH MY DREAM is

WORD OR AFFiRMATiON I WiLL FOCUS ON

to KEEP MY DREAMS ALiVE

MAY 2023

MONDAY
15

TUESDAY
16

WEDNESDAY
17

THURSDAY
18

FRIDAY
19

● New Moon

SATURDAY
20

Armed Forces Day (USA)

SUNDAY
21

MAY 2023

S	M	T	W	T	F	S
	1	2	3	4	5	6
7	8	9	10	11	12	13
14	15	16	17	18	19	20
21	22	23	24	25	26	27
28	29	30	31			

JUNE 2023

S	M	T	W	T	F	S
				1	2	3
4	5	6	7	8	9	10
11	12	13	14	15	16	17
18	19	20	21	22	23	24
25	26	27	28	29	30	

APPRECIATE the GOOD

I SEND the following BLESSINGS to OTHERS
and TO the WORLD

I AM GRATEFUL for

LOVE MYSELF DEEPLY

I AM PROUD of MYSELF for

I AM LETTING GO of

MANIFEST and ATTRACT

I LISTEN DEEPLY then ASK CLEARLY for MY HEART'S DESIRES.
I AM MANIFESTING THIS or SOMETHING BETTER...

VISUALIZE IT

I CLOSE MY EYES for 3 MINUTES and
IMAGINE HOW MY MANIFESTATION MIGHT
TASTE, LOOK, FEEL, SMELL, and SOUND
WHEN IT COMES TRUE.

TAKE INSPIRED ACTION

ONE ACTION I WILL TAKE in
ALIGNMENT WITH MY DREAM is

WORD OR AFFIRMATION I WILL FOCUS ON
to
KEEP MY DREAMS ALIVE

MAY 2023

MONDAY

22

Victoria Day (Canada)

TUESDAY

23

WEDNESDAY

24

THURSDAY

25

FRIDAY

26

MAY 2023
S M T W T F S
   1 2 3 4 5 6
7 8 9 10 11 12 13
14 15 16 17 18 19 20
21 22 23 24 25 26 27
28 29 30 31

SATURDAY

27

◑ First Quarter

JUNE 2023
S M T W T F S
            1 2 3
4 5 6 7 8 9 10
11 12 13 14 15 16 17
18 19 20 21 22 23 24
25 26 27 28 29 30

SUNDAY

28

APPRECIATE the GOOD

I SEND the fOLLOWiNG BLESSiNGS to OTHERS
and To the WORLD

I AM GRATEFUL for

LOVE MYSELF DEEPLY

I AM PROUD of MYSELF for

I AM LETTiNG GO of

MANiFEST and ATTRACT

I LiSTEN DEEPLY then ASK CLEARLY for MY HEART'S DESiRES.
I AM MANiFESTiNG THiS or SOMETHiNG BETTER...

ViSUALiZE iT

I CLOSE MY EYES for 3 MiNUTES and
IMAGiNE HOW MY MANiFESTATiON MiGHT
TASTE, LOOK, FEEL, SMELL, and SOUND
WHEN iT COMES TRUE.

TAKE INSPiRED ACTiON

ONE ACTiON I WiLL TAKE in
ALiGNMENT WiTH MY DREAM iS

WORD OR AFFiRMATiON I WiLL FOCUS ON

to KEEP MY DREAMS ALiVE

MONDAY

29

Memorial Day (USA) • Bank Holiday (UK)

TUESDAY

30

WEDNESDAY

31

THURSDAY

1

FRIDAY

2

MAY 2023

S	M	T	W	T	F	S
	1	2	3	4	5	6
7	8	9	10	11	12	13
14	15	16	17	18	19	20
21	22	23	24	25	26	27
28	29	30	31			

SATURDAY

3

JUNE 2023

S	M	T	W	T	F	S
				1	2	3
4	5	6	7	8	9	10
11	12	13	14	15	16	17
18	19	20	21	22	23	24
25	26	27	28	29	30	

SUNDAY

4

○ Full Moon

APPRECIATE the GOOD

I SEND the fOLLOWiNG BLESSiNGS to OTHeRS
and To the WORLD

I AM GRATefUL for

LOVE MYSelf DEEPLY

I AM PROUD of MYSelf for

I AM LETTiNG GO of

MANiFeST and ATTRACT

I LiSTEN DeePLY then ASK CLEARLY for MY HEART'S DeSiReS.
I AM MANiFeSTiNG THiS or SOMeTHiNG BeTTeR...

ViSUALiZe iT

I CLOSE MY EYES for 3 MiNUTeS and
IMAGiNe HOW MY MANiFeSTATiON MiGHT
TASTE, LOOK, feeL, SMELL, and SOUND
WHEN iT COMeS TRUE.

TAKe INSPiReD ACTION

One ACTiON I WiLL TAKe in
ALiGNMENT WiTH MY DReAM iS

WORD OR AFFiRMATION I WiLL FOCUS ON

to KEEP MY DReAMS ALiVE

June 2023

MONDAY
5
Queen's Birthday (NZ) • Bank Holiday (Ireland)

TUESDAY
6

WEDNESDAY
7

THURSDAY
8

FRIDAY
9

SATURDAY
10
◑ Last Quarter

SUNDAY
11

JUNE 2023

S	M	T	W	T	F	S
				1	2	3
4	5	6	7	8	9	10
11	12	13	14	15	16	17
18	19	20	21	22	23	24
25	26	27	28	29	30	

JULY 2023

S	M	T	W	T	F	S
						1
2	3	4	5	6	7	8
9	10	11	12	13	14	15
16	17	18	19	20	21	22
23	24	25	26	27	28	29
30	31					

APPRECIATE the GOOD

I SEND the following BLESSINGS to OTHERS
and To the WORLD

I AM GRATEFUL for

LOVE MYSELF DEEPLY

I AM PROUD of MYSELF for

I AM LETTING GO of

MANIFEST and ATTRACT

I LISTEN DEEPLY then ASK CLEARLY for MY HEART'S DESIRES.
I AM Manifesting THIS or SOMETHING BETTER...

VISUALIZE IT

I CLOSE MY EYES for 3 MINUTES and
IMAGINE HOW MY MANIFESTATION MIGHT
TASTE, LOOK, FEEL, SMELL, and SOUND
WHEN IT COMES TRUE.

TAKE INSPIRED ACTION

One ACTION I WILL TAKE in
ALIGNMENT WITH MY DREAM is

WORD OR AFFIRMATION I WILL FOCUS ON
to KEEP MY DREAMS ALIVE

June 2023

MONDAY
12
Queen's Birthday (Australia—except QLD, WA)

TUESDAY
13

WEDNESDAY
14
Flag Day (USA)

THURSDAY
15

FRIDAY
16

SATURDAY
17

JUNE 2023
S	M	T	W	T	F	S
				1	2	3
4	5	6	7	8	9	10
11	12	13	14	15	16	17
18	19	20	21	22	23	24
25	26	27	28	29	30	

SUNDAY
18
● New Moon
Father's Day (USA, Canada, Ireland, UK)

JULY 2023
S	M	T	W	T	F	S
						1
2	3	4	5	6	7	8
9	10	11	12	13	14	15
16	17	18	19	20	21	22
23	24	25	26	27	28	29
30	31					

APPRECIATE the GOOD

I SEND the fOLLOWING BLESSINGS to OTHERS
and TO the WORLD

I AM GRATEFUL for

LOVE MYSELF DEEPLY

I AM PROUD of MYSELF for

I AM LETTING GO of

MANIFEST and ATTRACT

I LISTEN DEEPLY then ASK CLEARLY for MY HEART'S DESIRES.
I AM MANIFESTING THIS or SOMETHING BETTER...

VISUALIZE IT

I CLOSE MY EYES for 3 MINUTES and
IMAGINE HOW MY MANIFESTATION MIGHT
TASTE, LOOK, FEEL, SMELL, and SOUND
WHEN IT COMES TRUE.

TAKE INSPIRED ACTION

ONE ACTION I WILL TAKE in
ALIGNMENT WITH MY DREAM is

WORD OR AFFIRMATION I WILL FOCUS ON
to KEEP MY DREAMS ALIVE

JUNE 2023

MONDAY
19

Juneteenth (USA)

TUESDAY
20

WEDNESDAY
21

Summer Solstice • National Indigenous Peoples Day (Canada)

THURSDAY
22

FRIDAY
23

SATURDAY
24

JUNE 2023
S	M	T	W	T	F	S
				1	2	3
4	5	6	7	8	9	10
11	12	13	14	15	16	17
18	19	20	21	22	23	24
25	26	27	28	29	30	

SUNDAY
25

JULY 2023
S	M	T	W	T	F	S
						1
2	3	4	5	6	7	8
9	10	11	12	13	14	15
16	17	18	19	20	21	22
23	24	25	26	27	28	29
30	31					

APPRECIATE the GOOD

I SEND the FOLLOWING BLESSINGS to OTHERS and To the WORLD

I AM GRATEFUL for

LOVE MYSELF DEEPLY

I AM PROUD of MYSELF for

I AM LETTING GO of

MANIFEST and ATTRACT

I LISTEN DEEPLY then ASK CLEARLY for MY HEART'S DESIRES.
I AM MANIFESTING THIS or SOMETHING BETTER...

VISUALIZE iT

I CLOSE MY EYES for 3 MINUTES and IMAGINE HOW MY MANIFESTATION MIGHT TASTE, LOOK, FEEL, SMELL, and SOUND WHEN iT COMES TRUE.

TAKE INSPIRED ACTION

ONE ACTION I WILL TAKE in ALIGNMENT WITH MY DREAM is

WORD OR AFFIRMATION I WILL FOCUS ON to KEEP MY DREAMS ALIVE

June-July 2023

MONDAY

26

◑ First Quarter

TUESDAY

27

WEDNESDAY

28

Eid al-Adha

THURSDAY

29

FRIDAY

30

JUNE 2023

S	M	T	W	T	F	S
				1	2	3
4	5	6	7	8	9	10
11	12	13	14	15	16	17
18	19	20	21	22	23	24
25	26	27	28	29	30	

SATURDAY

1

Canada Day

JULY 2023

S	M	T	W	T	F	S
						1
2	3	4	5	6	7	8
9	10	11	12	13	14	15
16	17	18	19	20	21	22
23	24	25	26	27	28	29
30	31					

SUNDAY

2

APPRECIATE the GOOD

I SEND the FOLLOWING BLESSINGS to OTHERS
and To the WORLD

I AM GRATEFUL for

LOVE MYSELF DEEPLY

I AM PROUD of MYSELF for

I AM LETTING GO of

MANIFEST and ATTRACT

I LISTEN DEEPLY then ASK CLEARLY for MY HEART'S DESIRES.
I AM MANIFESTING THIS or SOMETHING BETTER...

VISUALIZE IT

I CLOSE MY EYES for 3 MINUTES and
IMAGINE HOW MY MANIFESTATION MIGHT
TASTE, LOOK, FEEL, SMELL, and SOUND
WHEN IT COMES TRUE.

TAKE INSPIRED ACTION

ONE ACTION I WILL TAKE in
ALIGNMENT WITH MY DREAM is

WORD OR AFFIRMATION I WILL FOCUS ON

to KEEP MY DREAMS ALIVE

JULY 2023

MONDAY
3

O Full Moon

TUESDAY
4

Independence Day (USA)

WEDNESDAY
5

THURSDAY
6

FRIDAY
7

JULY 2023

S	M	T	W	T	F	S
						1
2	3	4	5	6	7	8
9	10	11	12	13	14	15
16	17	18	19	20	21	22
23	24	25	26	27	28	29
30	31					

SATURDAY
8

AUGUST 2023

S	M	T	W	T	F	S
		1	2	3	4	5
6	7	8	9	10	11	12
13	14	15	16	17	18	19
20	21	22	23	24	25	26
27	28	29	30	31		

SUNDAY
9

APPRECIATE the GOOD

I SEND the fOLLOWING BLESSINGS to OTHERS and To the WORLD

I AM GRATEFUL for

LOVE MYSELF DEEPLY

I AM PROUD of MYSELF for

I AM LETTING GO of

MANiFest and ATTRACT

I LISTEN DEEPLY then ASK CLEARLY for MY HEART'S DESIRES.
I AM MANifesting THIS or SOMETHING BETTER...

ViSUALiZE iT

I CLOSE MY EYES for 3 MINUTES and IMAGINE HOW MY MANiFESTATION MiGHT TASTE, LOOK, FEEL, SMELL, and SOUND WHEN iT COMES TRUE.

TAKE INSPIRED ACTION

ONE ACTION I WILL TAKE in ALIGNMENT WITH MY DREAM iS

WORD OR AFFIRMATION I WILL FOCUS ON to KEEP MY DREAMS ALIVE

JULY 2023

MONDAY

10

◑ Last Quarter

TUESDAY

11

WEDNESDAY

12

THURSDAY

13

FRIDAY

14

SATURDAY

15

SUNDAY

16

JULY 2023

S	M	T	W	T	F	S
						1
2	3	4	5	6	7	8
9	10	11	12	13	14	15
16	17	18	19	20	21	22
23	24	25	26	27	28	29
30	31					

AUGUST 2023

S	M	T	W	T	F	S
		1	2	3	4	5
6	7	8	9	10	11	12
13	14	15	16	17	18	19
20	21	22	23	24	25	26
27	28	29	30	31		

APPRECIATE the GOOD

I SEND the fOLLOWING BLESSINGS to OTHERS and TO the WORLD

I AM GRATEFUL for

LOVE MYSELF DEEPLY

I AM PROUD of MYSELF for

I AM LETTING GO of

MANIFEST and ATTRACT

I LISTEN DEEPLY then ASK CLEARLY for MY HEART'S DESIRES.
I AM MANIFESTING THIS or SOMETHING BETTER...

VISUALIZE IT

I CLOSE MY EYES for 3 MINUTES and IMAGINE HOW MY MANIFESTATION MIGHT TASTE, LOOK, FEEL, SMELL, and SOUND WHEN IT COMES TRUE.

TAKE INSPIRED ACTION

ONE ACTION I WILL TAKE IN ALIGNMENT WITH MY DREAM IS

WORD OR AFFIRMATION I WILL FOCUS ON to KEEP MY DREAMS ALIVE

JULY 2023

MONDAY
17

● New Moon

TUESDAY
18

WEDNESDAY
19

THURSDAY
20

FRIDAY
21

JULY 2023

S	M	T	W	T	F	S
						1
2	3	4	5	6	7	8
9	10	11	12	13	14	15
16	17	18	19	20	21	22
23	24	25	26	27	28	29
30	31					

AUGUST 2023

S	M	T	W	T	F	S
		1	2	3	4	5
6	7	8	9	10	11	12
13	14	15	16	17	18	19
20	21	22	23	24	25	26
27	28	29	30	31		

SATURDAY
22

SUNDAY
23

APPRECIATE the GOOD

I SEND the fOllOWING BLESSINGS to OTHERs and TO the WORLD

I AM GRATEFUL for

LOVE myself DEEPLY

I AM PROUD of MYSELf for

I AM LETTING GO of

MANIFEST and ATTRACT

I LISTEN DEEPLY then ASK CLEARLY for MY HEART'S DESIRES.
I AM MANIFESTING THIS or SOMETHING BETTER...

VISUALIZE iT

I CLOSE MY EYES for 3 MINUTES and IMAGINE HOW MY MANIFESTATION MIGHT TASTE, LOOK, FEEL, SMELL, and SOUND WHEN iT COMES TRUE.

TAKE INSPIRED ACTION

ONE ACTION I WiLL TAKE in ALIGNMENT WITH MY DREAM is

WORD OR AFFIRMATION I WILL FOCUS ON to KEEP MY DREAMS ALiVE

JULY 2023

MONDAY
24

TUESDAY
25

◐ First Quarter

WEDNESDAY
26

THURSDAY
27

FRIDAY
28

SATURDAY
29

SUNDAY
30

JULY 2023

S	M	T	W	T	F	S
						1
2	3	4	5	6	7	8
9	10	11	12	13	14	15
16	17	18	19	20	21	22
23	24	25	26	27	28	29
30	31					

AUGUST 2023

S	M	T	W	T	F	S
		1	2	3	4	5
6	7	8	9	10	11	12
13	14	15	16	17	18	19
20	21	22	23	24	25	26
27	28	29	30	31		

APPRECIATE the GOOD

I SEND the fOllOWiNG BLESSiNGS tO OTHERS
and TO the WORLD

I AM GRATEFUL for

LOVE MYSELF DEEPLY

I AM PROUD of MYSELF for

I AM LETTiNG GO of

MANiFEST and ATTRACT

I LiSTEN DEEPLY then ASK CLEARLY for MY HEART'S DESiRES.
I AM MANifESTiNG THiS or SOMETHiNG BETTER...

ViSUALiZE iT

I CLOSE MY EYES for 3 MiNUTES and
IMAGiNE HOW MY MANifESTATiON MiGHT
TASTE, LOOK, FEEL, SMELL, and SOUND
WHEN iT COMES TRUE.

TAKE INSPiRED ACTiON

ONE ACTION I WiLL TAKE in
ALIGNMENT WiTH MY DREAM is

WORD OR AFFiRMATiON I WiLL FOCUS ON to KEEP MY DREAMS ALiVE

July-Aug 2023

MONDAY
31

TUESDAY
1

○ Full Moon

WEDNESDAY
2

THURSDAY
3

FRIDAY
4

JULY 2023

S	M	T	W	T	F	S
						1
2	3	4	5	6	7	8
9	10	11	12	13	14	15
16	17	18	19	20	21	22
23	24	25	26	27	28	29
30	31					

SATURDAY
5

AUGUST 2023

S	M	T	W	T	F	S
		1	2	3	4	5
6	7	8	9	10	11	12
13	14	15	16	17	18	19
20	21	22	23	24	25	26
27	28	29	30	31		

SUNDAY
6

APPRECIATE the GOOD

I SEND the FOLLOWING BLESSINGS to OTHERS
and TO the WORLD

I AM GRATEFUL for

LOVE MYSELF DEEPLY

I AM PROUD of MYSELF for

I AM LETTING GO of

MANIFEST and ATTRACT

I LISTEN DEEPLY then ASK CLEARLY for MY HEART'S DESIRES.
I AM MANIFESTING THIS or SOMETHING BETTER...

VISUALIZE IT

I CLOSE MY EYES for 3 MINUTES and
IMAGINE HOW MY MANIFESTATION MIGHT
TASTE, LOOK, FEEL, SMELL, and SOUND
WHEN IT COMES TRUE.

TAKE INSPIRED ACTION

ONE ACTION I WILL TAKE in
ALIGNMENT WITH MY DREAM IS

WORD OR AFFIRMATION I WILL FOCUS ON to KEEP MY DREAMS ALIVE

AuGUST 2023

MONDAY
7

Bank Holiday (Ireland, UK—Scotland, Australia—NSW) • Picnic Day (Australia—NT)

TUESDAY
8

◗ Last Quarter

WEDNESDAY
9

THURSDAY
10

FRIDAY
11

AUGUST 2023

S	M	T	W	T	F	S
		1	2	3	4	5
6	7	8	9	10	11	12
13	14	15	16	17	18	19
20	21	22	23	24	25	26
27	28	29	30	31		

SATURDAY
12

SEPTEMBER 2023

S	M	T	W	T	F	S
					1	2
3	4	5	6	7	8	9
10	11	12	13	14	15	16
17	18	19	20	21	22	23
24	25	26	27	28	29	30

SUNDAY
13

APPRECIATE the GOOD

I SEND the fOLLOWING BLESSINGS to OTHERS
and TO the WORLD

I AM GRATEFUL for

LOVE MYSELF DEEPLY

I AM PROUD of MYSELF for

I AM LETTING GO of

MANIFEST and ATTRACT

I LISTEN DEEPLY then ASK CLEARLY for MY HEART'S DESIRES.
I AM MANIFESTING THIS or SOMETHING BETTER...

VISUALIZE IT

I CLOSE MY EYES for 3 MINUTES and
IMAGINE HOW MY MANIFESTATION MIGHT
TASTE, LOOK, FEEL, SMELL, and SOUND
WHEN IT COMES TRUE.

TAKE INSPIRED ACTION

ONE ACTION I WILL TAKE in
ALIGNMENT WITH MY DREAM is

WORD OR AFFIRMATION I WILL FOCUS ON to KEEP MY DREAMS ALIVE

AuGUST 2023

MONDAY
14

TUESDAY
15

WEDNESDAY
16

● New Moon

THURSDAY
17

FRiDAY
18

SATURDAY
19

SUNDAY
20

APPRECIATE the GOOD

I SEND the fOLLOWING BLESSINGS to OTHERS
and TO the WORLD

I AM GRATEFUL for

LOVE MYSELF DEEPLY

I AM PROUD of MYSELF for

I AM LETTING GO of

MANiFest and ATTRACT

I LISTEN DEEPLY then ASK CLEARLY for MY HEART'S DESiRES.
I AM MAnifesting THiS or SOMETHiNG BETTeR...

ViSUALiZe iT

I CLOSE MY EYES for 3 MiNuteS and
IMAGiNE HOW MY MANifeSTATiON MiGHT
TASTE, LOOK, FeeL, SMELL, and SOUND
WHEN iT COMES TRUE.

TAKE iNSPiReD ACTiON

ONE ACTION I WiLL TAKE in
ALiGNMENT WiTH MY DREAM iS

WORD OR AFFiRMATiON I WiLL FOCUS ON
to KEEP MY DREAMS ALiVE

AUGUST 2023

MONDAY
21

TUESDAY
22

WEDNESDAY
23

THURSDAY
24

◑ First Quarter

FRIDAY
25

SATURDAY
26

SUNDAY
27

AUGUST 2023
S	M	T	W	T	F	S
		1	2	3	4	5
6	7	8	9	10	11	12
13	14	15	16	17	18	19
20	21	22	23	24	25	26
27	28	29	30	31		

SEPTEMBER 2023
S	M	T	W	T	F	S
					1	2
3	4	5	6	7	8	9
10	11	12	13	14	15	16
17	18	19	20	21	22	23
24	25	26	27	28	29	30

APPRECIATE the GOOD

I SEND the following BLESSINGS to OTHERS and To the WORLD

I AM GRATEFUL for

LOVE MYSELF DEEPLY

I AM PROUD of MYSELF for

I AM LETTING GO of

MANIFEST and ATTRACT

I LISTEN DEEPLY then ASK CLEARLY for MY HEART'S DESIRES.
I AM MANIFESTING THIS or SOMETHING BETTER...

VISUALIZE IT

I CLOSE MY EYES for 3 MINUTES and IMAGINE HOW MY MANIFESTATION MIGHT TASTE, LOOK, FEEL, SMELL, and SOUND WHEN IT COMES TRUE.

TAKE INSPIRED ACTION

ONE ACTION I WILL TAKE in ALIGNMENT WITH MY DREAM is

WORD OR AFFIRMATION I WILL FOCUS ON to KEEP MY DREAMS ALIVE

AuG-SeP 2023

MONDAY
28
Bank Holiday (UK—except Scotland)

TUESDAY
29

WEDNESDAY
30

THURSDAY
31
O Full Moon

FRIDAY
1

SATURDAY
2

SUNDAY
3
Father's Day (Australia, NZ)

AUGUST 2023

S	M	T	W	T	F	S
		1	2	3	4	5
6	7	8	9	10	11	12
13	14	15	16	17	18	19
20	21	22	23	24	25	26
27	28	29	30	31		

SEPTEMBER 2023

S	M	T	W	T	F	S
					1	2
3	4	5	6	7	8	9
10	11	12	13	14	15	16
17	18	19	20	21	22	23
24	25	26	27	28	29	30

APPRECIATE the GOOD

I SEND the FOLLOWING BLESSINGS to OTHERS
and TO the WORLD

I AM GRATEFUL for

LOVE MYSELF DEEPLY

I AM PROUD of MYSELF for

I AM LETTING GO of

MANIFEST and ATTRACT

I LISTEN DEEPLY then ASK CLEARLY for MY HEART'S DESIRES.
I AM MANIFESTING THIS or SOMETHING BETTER...

VISUALIZE IT

I CLOSE MY EYES for 3 MINUTES and
IMAGINE HOW MY MANIFESTATION MIGHT
TASTE, LOOK, FEEL, SMELL, and SOUND
WHEN IT COMES TRUE.

TAKE INSPIRED ACTION

ONE ACTION I WILL TAKE in
ALIGNMENT WITH MY DREAM IS

WORD OR AFFIRMATION I WILL FOCUS ON
to KEEP MY DREAMS ALIVE

SepTeMBeR 2023

MONDAY
4

Labor Day (USA, Canada)

TUESDAY
5

WEDNESDAY
6

◑ Last Quarter

THURSDAY
7

FRiDAY
8

SATURDAY
9

SUNDAY
10

SEPTEMBER 2023

S	M	T	W	T	F	S
					1	2
3	4	5	6	7	8	9
10	11	12	13	14	15	16
17	18	19	20	21	22	23
24	25	26	27	28	29	30

OCTOBER 2023

S	M	T	W	T	F	S
1	2	3	4	5	6	7
8	9	10	11	12	13	14
15	16	17	18	19	20	21
22	23	24	25	26	27	28
29	30	31				

APPRECIATE the GOOD

I SEND the following BLESSINGS to OTHERS and TO the WORLD

I AM GRATEFUL for

LOVE MYSELF DEEPLY

I AM PROUD of MYSELF for

I AM LETTING GO of

MANIFEST and ATTRACT

I LISTEN DEEPLY then ASK CLEARLY for MY HEART'S DESIRES.
I AM MANIFESTING THIS or SOMETHING BETTER...

VISUALIZE IT

I CLOSE MY EYES for 3 MINUTES and IMAGINE HOW MY MANIFESTATION MIGHT TASTE, LOOK, FEEL, SMELL, and SOUND WHEN IT COMES TRUE.

TAKE INSPIRED ACTION

ONE ACTION I WILL TAKE IN ALIGNMENT WITH MY DREAM IS

WORD OR AFFIRMATION I WILL FOCUS ON to KEEP MY DREAMS ALIVE

SePTeMBeR 2023

MONDAY
11

TUESDAY
12

WEDNESDAY
13

THURSDAY
14

FRiDAY
15

● New Moon
Rosh Hashanah (begins at sundown)

SATURDAY
16

SUNDAY
17

Rosh Hashanah ends

SEPTEMBER 2023
S	M	T	W	T	F	S
					1	2
3	4	5	6	7	8	9
10	11	12	13	14	15	16
17	18	19	20	21	22	23
24	25	26	27	28	29	30

OCTOBER 2023
S	M	T	W	T	F	S
1	2	3	4	5	6	7
8	9	10	11	12	13	14
15	16	17	18	19	20	21
22	23	24	25	26	27	28
29	30	31				

APPRECIATE the GOOD

I SEND the fOLLOWING BLESSINGS to OTHERS
and TO the WORLD

I AM GRATEFUL for

LOVE MYSELF DEEPLY

I AM PROUD of MYSELF for

I AM LETTING GO of

MANIFEST and ATTRACT

I LISTEN DEEPLY then ASK CLEARLY for MY HEART'S DESIRES.
I AM MANIFESTING THIS or SOMETHING BETTER...

VISUALIZE IT

I CLOSE MY EYES for 3 MINUTES and
IMAGINE HOW MY MANIFESTATION MIGHT
TASTE, LOOK, FEEL, SMELL, and SOUND
WHEN IT COMES TRUE.

TAKE INSPIRED ACTION

ONE ACTION I WILL TAKE in
ALIGNMENT WITH MY DREAM is

WORD OR AFFIRMATION I WILL FOCUS ON
to KEEP MY DREAMS ALIVE

SEPTEMBER 2023

MONDAY
18

TUESDAY
19

WEDNESDAY
20

THURSDAY
21

U.N. International Day of Peace

FRIDAY
22

◑ First Quarter

SATURDAY
23

Autumnal Equinox

SUNDAY
24

Yom Kippur (begins at sundown)

SEPTEMBER 2023

S	M	T	W	T	F	S
					1	2
3	4	5	6	7	8	9
10	11	12	13	14	15	16
17	18	19	20	21	22	23
24	25	26	27	28	29	30

OCTOBER 2023

S	M	T	W	T	F	S
1	2	3	4	5	6	7
8	9	10	11	12	13	14
15	16	17	18	19	20	21
22	23	24	25	26	27	28
29	30	31				

APPRECIATE the GOOD

I SEND the following BLESSINGS to OTHERS
and TO the WORLD

I AM GRATEFUL for

LOVE MYSELF DEEPLY

I AM PROUD of MYSELF for

I AM LETTING GO of

MANIFEST and ATTRACT

I LISTEN DEEPLY then ASK CLEARLY for MY HEART'S DESIRES.
I AM MANIFESTING THIS or SOMETHING BETTER...

VISUALIZE IT

I CLOSE MY EYES for 3 MINUTES and
IMAGINE HOW MY MANIFESTATION MIGHT
TASTE, LOOK, FEEL, SMELL, and SOUND
WHEN IT COMES TRUE.

TAKE INSPIRED ACTION

ONE ACTION I WILL TAKE in
ALIGNMENT WITH MY DREAM is

WORD OR AFFIRMATION I WILL FOCUS ON

to KEEP MY DREAMS ALIVE

Sep–Oct 2023

MONDAY
25

Queen's Birthday (Australia—WA)

TUESDAY
26

WEDNESDAY
27

THURSDAY
28

FRIDAY
29

○ Full Moon

SATURDAY
30

SEPTEMBER 2023

S	M	T	W	T	F	S
					1	2
3	4	5	6	7	8	9
10	11	12	13	14	15	16
17	18	19	20	21	22	23
24	25	26	27	28	29	30

SUNDAY
1

OCTOBER 2023

S	M	T	W	T	F	S
1	2	3	4	5	6	7
8	9	10	11	12	13	14
15	16	17	18	19	20	21
22	23	24	25	26	27	28
29	30	31				

APPRECIATE the GOOD

I SEND the FOLLOWING BLESSINGS to OTHERS and To the WORLD

I AM GRATEFUL for

LOVE MYSELF DEEPLY

I AM PROUD of MYSELF for

I AM LETTING GO of

MANIFEST and ATTRACT

I LISTEN DEEPLY then ASK CLEARLY for MY HEART'S DESIRES.
I AM MANIFESTING THIS or SOMETHING BETTER...

VISUALIZE IT

I CLOSE MY EYES for 3 MINUTES and IMAGINE HOW MY MANIFESTATION MIGHT TASTE, LOOK, FEEL, SMELL, and SOUND WHEN IT COMES TRUE.

TAKE INSPIRED ACTION

ONE ACTION I WILL TAKE in ALIGNMENT WITH MY DREAM is

WORD OR AFFIRMATION I WILL FOCUS ON to KEEP MY DREAMS ALIVE

OCTOBER 2023

MONDAY
2
Labour Day (Australia—ACT, SA, NSW) • Queen's Birthday (Australia—QLD)

TUESDAY
3

WEDNESDAY
4

THURSDAY
5

FRIDAY
6

◑ Last Quarter

SATURDAY
7

OCTOBER 2023

S	M	T	W	T	F	S
1	2	3	4	5	6	7
8	9	10	11	12	13	14
15	16	17	18	19	20	21
22	23	24	25	26	27	28
29	30	31				

SUNDAY
8

NOVEMBER 2023

S	M	T	W	T	F	S
			1	2	3	4
5	6	7	8	9	10	11
12	13	14	15	16	17	18
19	20	21	22	23	24	25
26	27	28	29	30		

APPRECIATE the GOOD

I SEND the following BLESSINGS to OTHERS
and TO the WORLD

I AM GRATEFUL for

LOVE MYSELF DEEPLY

I AM PROUD of MYSELF for

I AM LETTING GO of

MANIFEST and ATTRACT

I LISTEN DEEPLY then ASK CLEARLY for MY HEART'S DESIRES.
I AM MANIFESTING THIS or SOMETHING BETTER...

VISUALIZE IT

I CLOSE MY EYES for 3 MINUTES and
IMAGINE HOW MY MANIFESTATION MIGHT
TASTE, LOOK, FEEL, SMELL, and SOUND
WHEN IT COMES TRUE.

TAKE INSPIRED ACTION

ONE ACTION I WILL TAKE in
ALIGNMENT WITH MY DREAM is

WORD OR AFFIRMATION I WILL FOCUS ON
to KEEP MY DREAMS ALIVE

OCTOBER 2023

MONDAY
9
Columbus Day (USA) • Indigenous Peoples' Day (USA) • Thanksgiving (Canada)

TUESDAY
10

WEDNESDAY
11

THURSDAY
12

FRIDAY
13

OCTOBER 2023

S	M	T	W	T	F	S
1	2	3	4	5	6	7
8	9	10	11	12	13	14
15	16	17	18	19	20	21
22	23	24	25	26	27	28
29	30	31				

SATURDAY
14
● New Moon

NOVEMBER 2023

S	M	T	W	T	F	S
			1	2	3	4
5	6	7	8	9	10	11
12	13	14	15	16	17	18
19	20	21	22	23	24	25
26	27	28	29	30		

SUNDAY
15

APPRECIATE the GOOD

I SEND the FOLLOWING BLESSINGS to OTHERS
and TO the WORLD

I AM GRATEFUL for

LOVE MYSELF DEEPLY

I AM PROUD of MYSELF for

I AM LETTING GO of

MANIFEST and ATTRACT

I LISTEN DEEPLY then ASK CLEARLY for MY HEART'S DESIRES.
I AM MANIFESTING THIS or SOMETHING BETTER...

VISUALIZE IT

I CLOSE MY EYES for 3 MINUTES and
IMAGINE HOW MY MANIFESTATION MIGHT
TASTE, LOOK, FEEL, SMELL, and SOUND
WHEN IT COMES TRUE.

TAKE INSPIRED ACTION

ONE ACTION I WILL TAKE in
ALIGNMENT WITH MY DREAM is

WORD OR AFFIRMATION I WILL FOCUS ON
to KEEP MY DREAMS ALIVE

OCTOBER 2023

MONDAY
16

TUESDAY
17

WEDNESDAY
18

THURSDAY
19

FRIDAY
20

OCTOBER 2023

S	M	T	W	T	F	S
1	2	3	4	5	6	7
8	9	10	11	12	13	14
15	16	17	18	19	20	21
22	23	24	25	26	27	28
29	30	31				

SATURDAY
21

NOVEMBER 2023

S	M	T	W	T	F	S
			1	2	3	4
5	6	7	8	9	10	11
12	13	14	15	16	17	18
19	20	21	22	23	24	25
26	27	28	29	30		

SUNDAY
22

◑ First Quarter

APPRECIATE the GOOD

I SEND the FOLLOWING BLESSINGS to OTHERS
and TO the WORLD

I AM GRATEFUL for

LOVE MYSELF DEEPLY

I AM PROUD of MYSELF for

I AM LETTING GO of

MANIFEST and ATTRACT

I LISTEN DEEPLY then ASK CLEARLY for MY HEART'S DESIRES.
I AM MANIFESTING THIS or SOMETHING BETTER...

VISUALIZE iT

I CLOSE MY EYES for 3 MINUTES and
IMAGINE HOW MY MANIFESTATION MIGHT
TASTE, LOOK, FEEL, SMELL, and SOUND
WHEN iT COMES TRUE.

TAKE INSPIRED ACTION

ONE ACTION I WILL TAKE in
ALIGNMENT WITH MY DREAM is

WORD OR AFFIRMATION I WILL FOCUS ON

to KEEP MY DREAMS ALIVE

OCTOBER 2023

MONDAY
23
Labour Day (NZ)

TUESDAY
24
United Nations Day

WEDNESDAY
25

THURSDAY
26

FRIDAY
27

OCTOBER 2023
S M T W T F S
1 2 3 4 5 6 7
8 9 10 11 12 13 14
15 16 17 18 19 20 21
22 23 24 25 26 27 28
29 30 31

SATURDAY
28
O Full Moon

NOVEMBER 2023
S M T W T F S
1 2 3 4
5 6 7 8 9 10 11
12 13 14 15 16 17 18
19 20 21 22 23 24 25
26 27 28 29 30

SUNDAY
29

APPRECIATE the GOOD

I SEND the FOLLOWING BLESSINGS to OTHERS and To the WORLD

I AM GRATEFUL for

LOVE MYSELF DEEPLY

I AM PROUD of MYSELF for

I AM LETTING GO of

MANIFEST and ATTRACT

I LISTEN DEEPLY then ASK CLEARLY for MY HEART'S DESIRES.
I AM MANIFESTING THIS or SOMETHING BETTER...

VISUALIZE IT

I CLOSE MY EYES for 3 MINUTES and IMAGINE HOW MY MANIFESTATION MIGHT TASTE, LOOK, FEEL, SMELL, and SOUND WHEN IT COMES TRUE.

TAKE INSPIRED ACTION

ONE ACTION I WILL TAKE in ALIGNMENT WITH MY DREAM is

WORD OR AFFIRMATION I WILL FOCUS ON to KEEP MY DREAMS ALIVE

Oct-Nov 2023

MONDAY
30
Bank Holiday (Ireland)

TUESDAY
31
Halloween

WEDNESDAY
1

THURSDAY
2

FRIDAY
3

OCTOBER 2023

S	M	T	W	T	F	S
1	2	3	4	5	6	7
8	9	10	11	12	13	14
15	16	17	18	19	20	21
22	23	24	25	26	27	28
29	30	31				

SATURDAY
4

NOVEMBER 2023

S	M	T	W	T	F	S
			1	2	3	4
5	6	7	8	9	10	11
12	13	14	15	16	17	18
19	20	21	22	23	24	25
26	27	28	29	30		

SUNDAY
5
◑ Last Quarter
Daylight Saving Time ends (USA, Canada)

APPRECIATE the GOOD

I SEND the FOLLOWING BLESSINGS to OTHERS
and To the WORLD

I AM GRATEFUL for

LOVE MYSELF DEEPLY

I AM PROUD of MYSELF for

I AM LETTING GO of

MANIFEST and ATTRACT

I LISTEN DEEPLY then ASK CLEARLY for MY HEART'S DESIRES.
I AM MANIFESTING THIS or SOMETHING BETTER...

VISUALIZE iT

I CLOSE MY EYES for 3 MINUTES and
IMAGINE HOW MY MANIFESTATION MIGHT
TASTE, LOOK, FEEL, SMELL, and SOUND
WHEN iT COMES TRUE.

TAKE INSPIRED ACTION

ONE ACTION I WILL TAKE in
ALIGNMENT WITH MY DREAM is

WORD OR AFFIRMATION I WILL FOCUS ON to KEEP MY DREAMS ALIVE

November 2023

MONDAY
6

TUESDAY
7

Election Day (USA)

WEDNESDAY
8

THURSDAY
9

FRIDAY
10

NOVEMBER 2023

S	M	T	W	T	F	S
			1	2	3	4
5	6	7	8	9	10	11
12	13	14	15	16	17	18
19	20	21	22	23	24	25
26	27	28	29	30		

SATURDAY
11

Veterans Day (USA) • Remembrance Day (Canada, UK, Ireland, Australia)

DECEMBER 2023

S	M	T	W	T	F	S
					1	2
3	4	5	6	7	8	9
10	11	12	13	14	15	16
17	18	19	20	21	22	23
24	25	26	27	28	29	30
31						

SUNDAY
12

Diwali • Remembrance Sunday (UK, Ireland)

APPRECIATE the GOOD

I SEND the fOllOWING BLESSINGS to OTHERS
and TO the WORLD

I AM GRATEFUL for

LOVE MYSELF DEEPLY

I AM PROUD of MYSELF for

I AM LETTING GO of

MANiFest and ATTRACT

I LiSTEN DEEPLY then ASK CLEARLY for MY HEART'S DESiRES.
I AM MANifesTiNG THiS or SOMETHiNG BETTER...

ViSUALiZE iT

I CLOSE MY EYES for 3 MiNUTES and
IMAGiNE HOW MY MANiFESTATiON MiGHT
TASTE, LOOK, FEEL, SMELL, and SOUND
WHEN iT COMES TRUE.

TAKE iNSPiRED ACTiON

ONE ACTION I WiLL TAKE iN
ALiGNMENT WiTH MY DREAM iS

WORD OR AFFiRMATiON I WiLL FOCUS ON to KEEP MY DREAMS ALiVE

November 2023

MONDAY
13

● New Moon

TUESDAY
14

WEDNESDAY
15

THURSDAY
16

FRIDAY
17

NOVEMBER 2023

S	M	T	W	T	F	S
			1	2	3	4
5	6	7	8	9	10	11
12	13	14	15	16	17	18
19	20	21	22	23	24	25
26	27	28	29	30		

SATURDAY
18

DECEMBER 2023

S	M	T	W	T	F	S
					1	2
3	4	5	6	7	8	9
10	11	12	13	14	15	16
17	18	19	20	21	22	23
24	25	26	27	28	29	30
31						

SUNDAY
19

APPRECIATE the GOOD

I SEND the fOllOWING BLESSINGS to OTHERS
and TO the WORLD

I AM GRATEFUL for

LOVE MYSELF DEEPLY

I AM PROUD of MYSELF for

I AM LETTING GO of

MANIFEST and ATTRACT

I LISTEN DEEPLY then ASK CLEARLY for MY HEART'S DESIRES.
I AM MANIFESTING THIS or SOMETHING BETTER...

VISUALIZE IT

I CLOSE MY EYES for 3 MINUTES and
IMAGINE HOW MY MANIFESTATION MIGHT
TASTE, LOOK, FEEL, SMELL, and SOUND
WHEN IT COMES TRUE.

TAKE INSPIRED ACTION

ONE ACTION I WILL TAKE in
ALIGNMENT WITH MY DREAM is

WORD OR AFFIRMATION I WILL FOCUS ON to KEEP MY DREAMS ALIVE

NovemBeR 2023

TUESDAY
21

WEDNESDAY
22

THURSDAY
23

Thanksgiving (USA)

FRIDAY
24

NOVEMBER 2023

S	M	T	W	T	F	S
			1	2	3	4
5	6	7	8	9	10	11
12	13	14	15	16	17	18
19	20	21	22	23	24	25
26	27	28	29	30		

SATURDAY
25

DECEMBER 2023

S	M	T	W	T	F	S
					1	2
3	4	5	6	7	8	9
10	11	12	13	14	15	16
17	18	19	20	21	22	23
24	25	26	27	28	29	30
31						

SUNDAY
26

APPRECIATE the GOOD

I SEND the following BLESSINGS to OTHERS
and TO the WORLD

I AM GRATEFUL for

LOVE MYSELF DEEPLY

I AM PROUD of MYSELF for

I AM LETTING GO of

MANIFEST and ATTRACT

I LISTEN DEEPLY then ASK CLEARLY for MY HEART'S DESIRES.
I AM MANIFESTING THIS or SOMETHING BETTER...

VISUALIZE IT

I CLOSE MY EYES for 3 MINUTES and
IMAGINE HOW MY MANIFESTATION MIGHT
TASTE, LOOK, FEEL, SMELL, and SOUND
WHEN IT COMES TRUE.

TAKE INSPIRED ACTION

ONE ACTION I WILL TAKE in
ALIGNMENT WITH MY DREAM is

WORD OR AFFIRMATION I WILL FOCUS ON to KEEP MY DREAMS ALIVE

Nov-Dec 2023

MONDAY

27

O Full Moon

TUESDAY

28

WEDNESDAY

29

THURSDAY

30

St. Andrew's Day (UK)

FRIDAY

1

SATURDAY

2

SUNDAY

3

NOVEMBER 2023
S	M	T	W	T	F	S
			1	2	3	4
5	6	7	8	9	10	11
12	13	14	15	16	17	18
19	20	21	22	23	24	25
26	27	28	29	30		

DECEMBER 2023
S	M	T	W	T	F	S
					1	2
3	4	5	6	7	8	9
10	11	12	13	14	15	16
17	18	19	20	21	22	23
24	25	26	27	28	29	30
31						

APPRECIATE the GOOD

I SEND the FOLLOWING BLESSINGS to OTHERS
and TO the WORLD

I AM GRATEFUL for

LOVE MYSELF DEEPLY

I AM PROUD of MYSELF for

I AM LETTING GO of

MANIFEST and ATTRACT

I LISTEN DEEPLY then ASK CLEARLY for MY HEART'S DESIRES.
I AM MANIFESTING THIS or SOMETHING BETTER...

VISUALIZE IT

I CLOSE MY EYES for 3 MINUTES and
IMAGINE HOW MY MANIFESTATION MIGHT
TASTE, LOOK, FEEL, SMELL, and SOUND
WHEN IT COMES TRUE.

TAKE INSPIRED ACTION

ONE ACTION I WILL TAKE in
ALIGNMENT WITH MY DREAM is

WORD OR AFFIRMATION I WILL FOCUS ON
to KEEP MY DREAMS ALIVE

DeCeMBeR 2023

MONDAY
4

TUESDAY
5

◑ Last Quarter

WEDNESDAY
6

THURSDAY
7

Hanukkah (begins at sundown)

FRiDAY
8

DECEMBER 2023
S	M	T	W	T	F	S
					1	2
3	4	5	6	7	8	9
10	11	12	13	14	15	16
17	18	19	20	21	22	23
24	25	26	27	28	29	30
31						

SATURDAY
9

JANUARY 2024
S	M	T	W	T	F	S
	1	2	3	4	5	6
7	8	9	10	11	12	13
14	15	16	17	18	19	20
21	22	23	24	25	26	27
28	29	30	31			

SUNDAY
10

Human Rights Day

APPRECIATE the GOOD

I SEND the FOLLOWING BLESSINGS to OTHERS and TO the WORLD

I AM GRATEFUL for

LOVE MYSELF DEEPLY

I AM PROUD of MYSELF for

I AM LETTING GO of

MANiFEST and ATTRACT

I LISTEN DEEPLY then ASK CLEARLY for MY HEART'S DESiRES.
I AM MANIFESTING THIS or SOMETHING BETTER...

VISUALIZE iT

I CLOSE MY EYES for 3 MINUTES and IMAGINE HOW MY MANIFESTATION MIGHT TASTE, LOOK, FEEL, SMELL, and SOUND WHEN iT COMES TRUE.

TAKE INSPIRED ACTION

ONE ACTION I WILL TAKE in ALIGNMENT WITH MY DREAM iS

WORD OR AFFIRMATION I WILL FOCUS ON to KEEP MY DREAMS ALIVE

DeCeMBeR 2023

MONDAY

11

TUESDAY

12

● New Moon

WEDNESDAY

13

THURSDAY

14

FRiDAY

15

Hanukkah ends

SATURDAY

16

SUNDAY

17

DECEMBER 2023

S	M	T	W	T	F	S
					1	2
3	4	5	6	7	8	9
10	11	12	13	14	15	16
17	18	19	20	21	22	23
24	25	26	27	28	29	30
31						

JANUARY 2024

S	M	T	W	T	F	S
	1	2	3	4	5	6
7	8	9	10	11	12	13
14	15	16	17	18	19	20
21	22	23	24	25	26	27
28	29	30	31			

APPRECIATE the GOOD

I SEND the FOLLOWING BLESSINGS to OTHERS
and TO the WORLD

I AM GRATEFUL for

LOVE MYSELF DEEPLY

I AM PROUD of MYSELF for

I AM LETTING GO of

MANIFEST and ATTRACT

I LISTEN DEEPLY then ASK CLEARLY for MY HEART'S DESIRES.
I AM MANIFESTING THIS or SOMETHING BETTER...

VISUALIZE IT

I CLOSE MY EYES for 3 MINUTES and
IMAGINE HOW MY MANIFESTATION MIGHT
TASTE, LOOK, FEEL, SMELL, and SOUND
WHEN IT COMES TRUE.

TAKE INSPIRED ACTION

ONE ACTION I WILL TAKE IN
ALIGNMENT WITH MY DREAM IS

WORD OR AFFIRMATION I WILL FOCUS ON to KEEP MY DREAMS ALIVE

DeCeMBeR 2023

MONDAY

18

TUESDAY

19

◑ First Quarter

WEDNESDAY

20

THURSDAY

21

FRiDAY

22

Winter Solstice

SATURDAY

23

SUNDAY

24

Christmas Eve

APPRECIATE the GOOD

I SEND the fOLLOWiNG BLESSiNGS to OTHERS
and TO the WORLD

I AM GRATEFUL for

LOVE MYSELF DEEPLY

I AM PROUD of MYSELF for

I AM LETTiNG GO of

MANiFEST and ATTRACT

I LISTEN DEEPLY then ASK CLEARLY for MY HEART'S DESiRES.
I AM MANifESTiNG THiS or SOMETHiNG BETTER...

ViSUALiZE iT

I CLOSE MY EYES for 3 MiNUTES and
IMAGiNE HOW MY MANifESTATION MiGHT
TASTE, LOOK, FEEL, SMELL, and SOUND
WHEN iT COMES TRUE.

TAKE iNSPiRED ACTiON

ONE ACTiON I WILL TAKE iN
ALIGNMENT WITH MY DREAM iS

WORD OR AFFIRMATION I WILL FOCUS ON to KEEP MY DREAMS ALiVE

DeCeMBeR 2023

MONDAY
25

Christmas Day

TUESDAY
26

Kwanzaa begins (USA) • Boxing Day (Canada, NZ, UK, Australia—except SA)
St. Stephen's Day (Ireland) • Proclamation Day (Australia—SA)

WEDNESDAY
27

○ Full Moon

THURSDAY
28

FRiDAY
29

DECEMBER 2023

S	M	T	W	T	F	S
					1	2
3	4	5	6	7	8	9
10	11	12	13	14	15	16
17	18	19	20	21	22	23
24	25	26	27	28	29	30
31						

SATURDAY
30

JANUARY 2024

S	M	T	W	T	F	S
	1	2	3	4	5	6
7	8	9	10	11	12	13
14	15	16	17	18	19	20
21	22	23	24	25	26	27
28	29	30	31			

SUNDAY
31

2024 PLANNING

JANURY

_____

_____

_____

FEBRUARY

_____

_____

_____

MARCH

_____

_____

_____

APRIL

_____

_____

_____

MAY

_____

_____

_____

JUNE

_____

_____

_____

2024 PLANNING

JULY

AUGUST

SEPTEMBER

OCTOBER

NOVEMBER

DECEMBER

2022

JANUARY
S	M	T	W	T	F	S
						1
2	3	4	5	6	7	8
9	10	11	12	13	14	15
16	17	18	19	20	21	22
23	24	25	26	27	28	29
30	31					

FEBRUARY
S	M	T	W	T	F	S
		1	2	3	4	5
6	7	8	9	10	11	12
13	14	15	16	17	18	19
20	21	22	23	24	25	26
27	28					

MARCH
S	M	T	W	T	F	S
		1	2	3	4	5
6	7	8	9	10	11	12
13	14	15	16	17	18	19
20	21	22	23	24	25	26
27	28	29	30	31		

APRIL
S	M	T	W	T	F	S
					1	2
3	4	5	6	7	8	9
10	11	12	13	14	15	16
17	18	19	20	21	22	23
24	25	26	27	28	29	30

MAY
S	M	T	W	T	F	S
1	2	3	4	5	6	7
8	9	10	11	12	13	14
15	16	17	18	19	20	21
22	23	24	25	26	27	28
29	30	31				

JUNE
S	M	T	W	T	F	S
			1	2	3	4
5	6	7	8	9	10	11
12	13	14	15	16	17	18
19	20	21	22	23	24	25
26	27	28	29	30		

JULY
S	M	T	W	T	F	S
					1	2
3	4	5	6	7	8	9
10	11	12	13	14	15	16
17	18	19	20	21	22	23
24	25	26	27	28	29	30
31						

AUGUST
S	M	T	W	T	F	S
	1	2	3	4	5	6
7	8	9	10	11	12	13
14	15	16	17	18	19	20
21	22	23	24	25	26	27
28	29	30	31			

SEPTEMBER
S	M	T	W	T	F	S
				1	2	3
4	5	6	7	8	9	10
11	12	13	14	15	16	17
18	19	20	21	22	23	24
25	26	27	28	29	30	

OCTOBER
S	M	T	W	T	F	S
						1
2	3	4	5	6	7	8
9	10	11	12	13	14	15
16	17	18	19	20	21	22
23	24	25	26	27	28	29
30	31					

NOVEMBER
S	M	T	W	T	F	S
		1	2	3	4	5
6	7	8	9	10	11	12
13	14	15	16	17	18	19
20	21	22	23	24	25	26
27	28	29	30			

DECEMBER
S	M	T	W	T	F	S
				1	2	3
4	5	6	7	8	9	10
11	12	13	14	15	16	17
18	19	20	21	22	23	24
25	26	27	28	29	30	31

2024

JANUARY

S	M	T	W	T	F	S
	1	2	3	4	5	6
7	8	9	10	11	12	13
14	15	16	17	18	19	20
21	22	23	24	25	26	27
28	29	30	31			

FEBRUARY

S	M	T	W	T	F	S
				1	2	3
4	5	6	7	8	9	10
11	12	13	14	15	16	17
18	19	20	21	22	23	24
25	26	27	28	29		

MARCH

S	M	T	W	T	F	S
					1	2
3	4	5	6	7	8	9
10	11	12	13	14	15	16
17	18	19	20	21	22	23
24	25	26	27	28	29	30
31						

APRIL

S	M	T	W	T	F	S
	1	2	3	4	5	6
7	8	9	10	11	12	13
14	15	16	17	18	19	20
21	22	23	24	25	26	27
28	29	30				

MAY

S	M	T	W	T	F	S
			1	2	3	4
5	6	7	8	9	10	11
12	13	14	15	16	17	18
19	20	21	22	23	24	25
26	27	28	29	30	31	

JUNE

S	M	T	W	T	F	S
						1
2	3	4	5	6	7	8
9	10	11	12	13	14	15
16	17	18	19	20	21	22
23	24	25	26	27	28	29
30						

JULY

S	M	T	W	T	F	S
	1	2	3	4	5	6
7	8	9	10	11	12	13
14	15	16	17	18	19	20
21	22	23	24	25	26	27
28	29	30	31			

AUGUST

S	M	T	W	T	F	S
				1	2	3
4	5	6	7	8	9	10
11	12	13	14	15	16	17
18	19	20	21	22	23	24
25	26	27	28	29	30	31

SEPTEMBER

S	M	T	W	T	F	S
1	2	3	4	5	6	7
8	9	10	11	12	13	14
15	16	17	18	19	20	21
22	23	24	25	26	27	28
29	30					

OCTOBER

S	M	T	W	T	F	S
		1	2	3	4	5
6	7	8	9	10	11	12
13	14	15	16	17	18	19
20	21	22	23	24	25	26
27	28	29	30	31		

NOVEMBER

S	M	T	W	T	F	S
					1	2
3	4	5	6	7	8	9
10	11	12	13	14	15	16
17	18	19	20	21	22	23
24	25	26	27	28	29	30

DECEMBER

S	M	T	W	T	F	S
1	2	3	4	5	6	7
8	9	10	11	12	13	14
15	16	17	18	19	20	21
22	23	24	25	26	27	28
29	30	31				

REFLECTIONS

DREAMS that HAVE MANIFESTED...

ReFLECTIONS

DREAMS that HAVE MANIFESTED...

REFLECTIONS

DREAMS that HAVE MANIFESTED...

ReFLECTIONS

DREAMS that HAVE MANifeSTeD...

REfLECTIONS

DREAMS that HAVE MANIFESTED...

ReFLECTIONS